Man Has Put
God on Trial and Found
Him Guilty!

In defense of God

E. C. MOSES JR.

ISBN: 978-1-963565-63-8 (Paperback)

ISBN: 978-1-963565-64-5 (eBook)

Library of Congress Control Number: 2024927420

Printed in the United States of America

Published by:

info@thequippyquill.com

(302) 295-2278

DEDICATION

I dedicate this to my Savior, the Lord Jesus Christ. Without His grace I would not be in a place to share this manuscript. It was by the hand of the Holy Spirit that I have been able to write this, and my praise and thanks go to the heavenly Father. I have attempted to demonstrate the love and grace He has shown to me in the space that follows. May your heart be blessed by this work.

I also would like to thank my wife, Nila. She is my true friend and my partner in life. She inspires me more than she realizes, and it is my heart's desire to bring happiness to her every day.

CONTENTS

Preface

Man has put God on trial and found Him guilty. Since the day that Adam turned his back on God by being disobedient, humankind has increasingly blamed God for their problems. It isn't that God is really to blame, but because there was a new landlord over the earth in the form of Satan, humankind has struggled to get back to the peace that was known long ago. In fact, it has been so long since that peace was known that we, collectively, have taken the path that we are in control of our destiny and God is just in the way. Every government on the planet is ruled by people who have their own agenda in mind. There is not one who is completely given over to biblical principles, allowing God Himself to guide their daily affairs. While Israel was founded as a nation of people by God, as a whole, they don't recognize Jesus Christ as the Messiah who was foretold by the prophets. They lost their place in the world for nearly two thousand years and were forced to live without a national place to call home. That home has since been restored, but the turmoil of the region keeps them ever on edge to protect those borders.

The United States of America was founded on Judeo-Christian principles way back in the 1700s. The founding fathers of this nation knew that as long as we followed these principles, God would bless this nation. The leaders and the people of the newly established country understood this and wholeheartedly lived out each day in submission to and dependence upon God. As this nation grew and the blessing of God became more evident, the prosperity of this country grew. People around the world began to recognize the United States as a place where they could come and start their lives over and also find that prosperity. As the United States became established as a force to be reckoned with, we were called upon for assistance by weaker nations looking for justice in an evil world. Finally, the day came when the United States was recognized by the world as the most powerful nation on the planet, ever.

Unfortunately, the pride and arrogance of this nation's leaders also grew. They became puffed up with pride, with the industries' advances, and with the wealth that was being generated. We were officially the leading nation of the world, and our leaders thought nobody could stop us from achieving anything we wanted. They were convinced that no country could mount a force that would dare attack this country on its own soil. The leadership of the United States began to review the foundational principles that started this nation and thus, made decisions to change those outdated and archaic ideas. The recognition of God and the ability to pray in schools was removed first. Some years later, it was made legal that if a woman did not want to bring her child to term, she could abort that baby without retribution or punishment. This nation decided that it no longer needed God or His rules guiding our legal system. The leadership decided that we were strong enough to make our own name and sustain ourselves and be captains of our own destiny.

The United States has put God on trial and consistently finds Him guilty of interfering with our ability to govern ourselves as we see fit. In times of calamity, damage is attributed to acts of God. When a death of a loved one occurs, it is said that God took them before we were ready for them to go. This same mentality holds true throughout the world's nations. Those who recognize that God does exist do so in passing but without any solid commitment to His ways.

Many other nations just add Him to the list of deities that can be found in the land. He is no different than the many gods they worship, hoping that one of them will hear their cry and answer their needs. Then there are a number of nations that boldly lay claim that God doesn't exist or that He is simply a lie fabricated by the nation of Israel.

He is being held in the same contempt as an absentee father, one who has abandoned his children and left them to fend for themselves. He is blamed for every bad thing that happens around the world, even in countries that officially refuse to recognize Him. Volcanic eruptions laying waste to the landscape, hurricanes decimating coasts, and earthquakes destroying the countryside are all blamed on God. Famine, pestilence, and disease are all blamed on God. When blessings do come, the people say, "We did this, and we did it by ourselves."

The following has been written as a defense of God's love and desire to be with man. This was done to demonstrate that since man fell from grace, God the Father has been working on His plan to restore humankind to its rightful place with Him.

CHAPTER 1

———— ·✖· ————

Man Be

———— ·✖· ————

God the Father wants to spend time with you. The Creator of the heavens—the one who made the stars and flung them into the vastness of space and called to order the expanse of the universe—wants to get to know you. The Lord of all that there is—the one who designed every living thing and placed them onto this planet that we call Earth—has a special place in His heart for you. After He prepared the earth, our home, so that it was perfect, and after He inspected every little detail and declared it good, it was then that He determined it was time for something truly special. In Genesis 1:26 it is stated, "Then God said, 'Let Us make man in Our image, according to Our likeness; let them have dominion over the fish of the sea, over the birds of the air, and over the cattle, over all the earth and over every creeping thing that creeps on the earth.'"

This was unprecedented in the eternity of heaven! Never in all of the heavenly beings that had been created was there a creature that was made after the likeness of God. Never was there a being made that was given dominion such as man. Never was there a being that was given the breath of life, the nephesh, from God's own nostrils. We were given a living soul. We were given the ability of God Himself, for we were made in His image and after His likeness. He bestowed upon us the ability to create other beings like ourselves—ones who would have eternal presence before God Himself. No other being has this gift. We were given the freedom of making our own decisions and our own choices. We were allowed to freely love our Creator, not out of strict obedience or out of a predefined ordinance but out of a pure desire to love back the one who loved us.

His desire is to walk with you, to listen to your stories, and to share in your wonder as you take in each day. He did that in the beginning with Adam and Eve. He came and walked with them in the cool of the day to spend quality one-on-one time with both of them. Unfortunately, a day came when that closeness was lost. Because we have the unique ability to make up our minds to follow our own will and make our own choices, a day came when the wrong choice was made.

That decision separated all of humankind from God our Father. At that point, we, the whole of humankind, were removed from the presence of God. It has been taught that it was a punishment for disobedience. I submit to you that there was a different reason for Him to separate us from His presence. Consider the idea that it was done for our protection. A holy God, one of such majesty, could not risk letting us come into His presence and be destroyed by that pure holiness. We were, at that point, full of sin. Sin cannot stand in the presence of God and survive. His love was so pure and so real that He had to separate Himself from us so we could be preserved until His plan of restoration could be fully realized and we could be redeemed.

That redemption came through His Son, His only begotten Son—the one who was there when all that we know around us was brought into existence and the one through whom all things were created. At the moment Adam committed high treason and disobeyed God by eating the fruit of the only tree that he was told not to eat from, that plan was put into action. Genesis 3:15 says, "And I will put enmity between you and the woman, and between your seed and her Seed; He shall bruise your head, and you shall bruise His heel." God was speaking to the Serpent, the highest of the order of the animal kingdom—the one that had allowed Satan to enter into it and tempt Eve into disobeying the command to not eat from the Tree of Knowledge of Good and Evil. Enmity is a feeling of intense hostility, and it is to be actively opposed to someone or something. So God told Satan that He was going to put intense hostility between him and the woman and between her offspring and his. This was the foretelling of the birth of Jesus and the hostility that would exist between Him and the world, which was filled with the sinful children of humankind who now belonged to Satan because of Adam's actions.

CHAPTER 2

The Tempter

Satan desires to take God's throne, to rule over all that has been created, and to have that worship given to him. He wants to have us do what we were given the freedom to do—to openly love and worship our Creator—but to instead direct that love and worship to him. It is his desire to be the recipient of that affection. But any person who is forced to give obeisance to a master is in reality a slave. There isn't a freedom to show affection willingly. It is forced or required, and when it isn't given, punishment is doled out. Blame is cast, and pain becomes a close acquaintance. We are the focal point of God's affection. All that exists was put there for our benefit. Because of this and the fact God gave us the right of free will—to love whom we choose and to ultimately decide for ourselves where we will spend eternity—Satan hates us. Because of that intense hatred, he wants to destroy this prize—this object of God's affection.

Satan was once known as Lucifer or "son of the morning," which means "light bearer." Isaiah 14:12–15 describes him saying in his heart that he was going to make himself like the Most High (God), but because of that intent, he was cast out of heaven and fell like lightning. He, Satan, no longer has the option to be forgiven. He initiated his own punishment and eternal damnation because of pride. When God created Lucifer, he was the signet of perfection. He was the highest creature that the Lord God had created. He was full of wisdom and perfect in beauty. He was absolutely stunning to look at, and music poured out from him when he moved. His description can be found in Ezekiel 28:12–19.

Son of man, take up a lamentation for the king of Tyre, and say to him, "Thus says the Lord God: 'You were the seal of perfection, Full of wisdom and perfect in beauty. You were in Eden, the garden of God; Every precious stone was your covering: The sardius, topaz, and diamond, beryl, onyx, and jasper, sapphire, turquoise, and emerald with gold. The workmanship of your timbrels and pipes was prepared for you on the day you were created. You were the anointed cherub who covers; I established you; you were on the holy mountain of God; you walked back and forth in the midst of fiery stones. You were perfect in your ways from the day you were created, till iniquity was found in you. By the abundance of your trading, you became filled with violence within, and you sinned; therefore, I cast you as a profane thing out of the mountain of God; and I destroyed you, O covering cherub, from the midst of the fiery stones. Your heart was lifted up because of your beauty; You corrupted your wisdom for the sake of your splendor; I cast you to the ground, I laid you before kings, that they might gaze at you. You defiled your sanctuaries by the multitude of your iniquities, by the iniquity of your trading; therefore, I brought fire from your midst; It devoured you, and I turned you to ashes upon the earth in the sight of all who saw you. All who knew you among the peoples are astonished at you; you have become a horror, and shall be no more forever.'"

This passage also describes how that beauty was taken away. A fire burned from within him and destroyed that brilliance and turned it to ash. It boils down to pride. He thought himself above all that was created but seemed to forget that he too was created. That selfish pride cost him his position with God in heaven. Because he was one of three archangels with a host of angelic beings under his authority, when he fell, they fell also. Responsibility falls to the head of the family, or order, to see to it that those put under their care are shown the way. When the head or leader is blessed, all of those under that responsibility are also blessed. But when the leader becomes corrupt and falls, all of those under that leadership fall as well.

CHAPTER 3

The Fall

We, humankind, started in perfect relationship with our Father. He, God the Father, is the ultimate family man and the model from which all people should draw their actions and behaviors. As the Creator of the universe, the Holy God of all there is. His very nature causes every single thing that exists to bow in worship and in submission to Him. But He wanted more. He wanted a being that wanted to love Him. He wanted a family. We were made to love Him openly, freely, and with everything that is in us. You don't have to look far to understand this concept. Look at babies and toddlers. They just love their parents. It is a part of them to love regardless of whether they receive any material property. They just want to love and be loved. It's plain to see how that same behavior is what God the Father so desires in a relationship with us.

Adam was given complete dominion over everything, so in essence, it was his kingdom. He was given only one rule that he could not break. Satan systematically went after this kingdom to usurp it from Adam. His intent was to take and make use of Adam's authority and trick him into giving that authority over so that he, Satan, would be the ruler of the kingdom. The serpent was first. Genesis 3:1 says that the serpent was more subtle than any of the beasts of the field. According to the Merriam-Webster Dictionary, Subtle indicates having a perceptive or refined insight and ability to penetrate deeply and thoroughly. So one could take this to mean that the serpent was able to make refined judgments, was intelligent and had keen insight. This creature was the highest of the animal kingdom. It makes sense that Satan would start here. Gain control of the highest of the order, and control of the rest will follow. Adam and Eve had a relationship with the animals. In Genesis 2:19–20 God brought the animals and birds to the man to see what he would name them; and whatever he called them, that was its name. It would seem that the creatures all understood him and accepted their names. It is not a far stretch to imagine that Adam, who was given dominion over all of the earth and everything within it, could communicate with his subjects and his subjects understood him. They accepted his leadership and received his words as the final say. So when the serpent spoke to the woman in Genesis 3:1–5, it would be reasonable to accept that the serpent and Eve were truly having a conversation.

The serpent allowed Satan to use his body as a means to speak to Eve. Satan took the words that God had spoken and twisted them just enough to cause Eve to wonder in her mind and question the command that had been given. Verses 4 and 5 state, "Then the serpent said to the woman, 'You will not surely die. For God knows that in the day you eat of it your eyes will be opened, and you will be like God, knowing good and evil.'" Let's look at this conversation a bit closer. In Genesis 2:16–17 God commanded the man, "Of every tree of the garden you may freely eat; but of the tree of the knowledge of good and evil you shall not eat, for in the day that you eat of it you shall surely die." A command was given, and the consequences were spelled out if that command was broken. Pretty straightforward, it would seem. Satan said, "You will not surely die," calling God a liar and challenging His authority over Adam and Eve. He further stated that their eyes would be opened, and they would be like God. Well in Genesis 1:26–27 God said, "Let us make man in our image, in our likeness," which means that we were already like God. So now Satan was saying that the only way to be like God was to disobey Him and eat the fruit they were told not to eat. All children desire to be like their parents. They spend hours of make believe playtime pretending to be just like their mom or dad, dressing up like them, saying things like them, acting out their behaviors as they interpret them to be. So here Eve was presented with false facts that played on her emotions. She responded to the information in a manner that is consistent with how so many children behave today when challenged that they are not like their mom or dad. Someone they know states that they are not like their parent unless they commit an action, which they already know they are not supposed to do. But the desire to be like dad drives the little boy to prove to the challenger that he is indeed like his dad. It becomes an act of accepting a lie and depending on one's pride to prove it wrong. Eve was told that in order to be like God, she would have to eat the fruit that she already knew she wasn't supposed to eat. But he drew her attention to it in Genesis 3:6: "So when the woman saw that the tree was good for food, that it was pleasant to the eyes, and a tree desirable to make one wise, she took of its fruit and ate."

We were made as visual creatures, taking in what we see with our eyes and enjoying the beauty of it. Everything God made was good and was done for our benefit. Genesis 2:9 says:

And out of the ground the Lord God made every tree grow that is pleasant to the sight and good for food. The tree of life was also in the midst of the garden, and the tree of the knowledge of good and evil.

So Satan drew Eve's attention to what he already knew she was designed to see—the fruit that was pleasing to the eye and good for food. When raising young children, sometimes the best way to keep them from trouble is to not let them see the very things that will draw them into trouble. As they get a bit older, we begin to teach them self-control. We teach them how to restrain themselves from certain actions that would bring harm to them. Since Adam and Eve were not young children and they were made in God's image, following the command to not partake of that one fruit should have been an easy task to keep. In fact, it didn't have to come to this at all because Adam was warned in Genesis 1:28 when God said to "fill the earth and subdue it." If Adam was the rightful ruler and there was no sin present, why would he have to subdue the earth? It seems that God was warning him, "Adam, there will be trouble coming along. You are going to have to put it down, take control over it, and not let it take hold." In other words, "Snake coming! You better watch out—that rascal needs to be kept in line!" From the beginning, Adam had been given all he needed to be able to keep his rule. He didn't listen very well. In fact, he was present the entire time that Satan was taking authority over his dominion. Genesis 3:6 states, "She also gave some to her husband, who was with her, and he ate it." Adam was standing right there the whole time, and when she handed him some of the fruit, he didn't protest. He didn't question what was going on; he just went ahead and ate it. You see, they were always together. Genesis 2:24 says, "Therefore, a man shall leave his father and mother and be joined to his wife, and they shall become one flesh." In Genesis 2:18, God said "It is not good that the man should be alone; I will make him a helper comparable to him." It was not God's intent for man to be alone but to have a helper, one who comes alongside and provides support, so that he would be able to walk through life in a loving relationship both physically and spiritually.

It was Adam's responsibility to teach Eve all he had been taught by God the Father. It was his responsibility to see to it that he and Eve became as one. Adam was given the dominion and the responsibility to protect it. That is why God told him to subdue the earth. Subdue means to bring under control or overcome. The very moment that Satan began to entice the serpent, Adam should have stepped up and taken control of the situation and thrown Satan out of there. But he didn't. Next, through the serpent, Satan began enticing Eve. All Adam had to do was speak and Satan would have been out of there. After all, he had the very nature of God within him. God spoke and the heavens came into existence. Adam was made in God's likeness, so it stands to reason that had he spoken with that likeness, God would have backed him up, and whatever he would have said would have come to pass. But Adam just stood by and watched without uttering a word. Last, Eve handed him a piece of the fruit, and again, all he had to do was say no. He could have cast it aside and not disobeyed God's command. Unfortunately, we are here today suffering from the results of his actions so many thousands of years ago.

CHAPTER 4

The Consequences

There is something that you need to take note of in this series of actions: it was not until Adam disobeyed and ate the fruit that both of them were affected. Genesis 3:7 states, "Then the eyes of both of them were opened, and they knew that they were naked; and they sewed fig leaves together and made themselves coverings." You see, Adam held the authority and responsibility for all of their actions. When he sinned, then everyone, and everything, was affected. God came looking for Adam and Eve so they could enjoy their evening walk together. But they were hiding from Him. Adam said in Genesis 3:10, "So he said, 'I heard Your voice in the garden, and I was afraid because I was naked; and I hid myself.'" When asked who told him he was naked, well, the blame game began. Adam blamed his disobedience on Eve. "She gave me some of the fruit, and I ate it; it's her fault." Eve said, "The serpent deceived me, and I ate." For the first time in their lives, they experienced fear and didn't know how to deal with it.

God first dealt with the serpent and his punishment. Genesis 3:14–15 says:

> *So the Lord God said to the serpent: "Because you have done this, you are cursed more than all cattle, and more than every beast of the field; On your belly you shall go, and you shall eat dust all the days of your life. And I will put enmity between you and the woman, and between your seed and her Seed; He shall bruise your head, and you shall bruise His heel.*

We all were made from the dust of the earth, and that includes the birds and animals. Once the lifeblood stops flowing and a creature dies, it decomposes and returns to the earth. At the time of the garden, all animals and birds ate from the green vegetation and the trees and the fruit that was produced by them. Genesis 1:30 states:

> *Also, to every beast of the earth, to every bird of the air, and to everything that creeps on the*

earth, in which there is life, I have given every
green herb for food"; and it was so.

This curse that was put upon the serpent at that point removed it from eating plants and caused it to now have to take a life in order to live itself. It had to kill another creature and then swallow that creature whole in order for it to continue to live. Furthermore, God took away its arms and legs and forced it to crawl on its belly. It went from highest to lowest in the breath of two sentences. It was very much like the fate that met Satan. He went from highest to lowest in the span of a sentence or two. In fact, it is recorded that he fell like lightning from heaven in Luke 10:18. We have all seen how fast lightning can light up the sky. That is how fast Lucifer, son of the morning, lit up the sky on his way down. Keep in mind that his actions not only affected him but those he was in charge of. Revelation 12:9 reads, "So the great dragon was cast out, that serpent of old, called the Devil and Satan, who deceives the whole world; he was cast to the earth, and his angels were cast out with him." With leadership and authority comes responsibility for those you are in charge of. Your actions affect their fate. That is God's way; it is how He designed things.

After He dealt with the serpent, He turned to Eve.

To the woman He said: "I will greatly multiply your sorrow and your conception; in pain you shall bring forth children; your desire shall be for your husband, and he shall rule over you." (Genesis 3:16)

For those who have had opportunity to witness how various members of the animal kingdom give birth to their offspring, they don't go through the same level of intensity as women do. Many of the animals in the wild are able to give birth, clean the baby up, and go about the business of living quite rapidly, seemingly without much pain at all. Not so for women because of this disobedience that Eve committed. In addition to that, her desire was to be for her husband. A longing would be in a woman's heart to have a husband, to be joined to a man. Furthermore, he would rule over, have dominion over her. This change was to have impact that is felt now with great contentions.

Adam had to stand there, watch, and listen as God told each of these two who were under his rule and protection what their fate would be and wait for his. In Genesis 3:17–19, it came.

Then to Adam He said, "Because you have heeded the voice of your wife, and have eaten from the tree of which I commanded you, saying, 'You shall not eat of it': "Cursed is the ground for your sake; In toil you shall eat of it All the days of your life. Both thorns and thistles it shall bring forth for you, and you shall eat the herb of the field. In the sweat of your face you shall eat bread till you return to the ground, for out of it you were taken; For dust you are, and to dust you shall return."

After this, God made garments for them out of skin and clothed them. The first sacrifice was committed. Animals had to be slain, their lives given, and their skin used to provide clothing for Adam and Eve. The next action taken by God must have been one of the hardest things to do as a Father. He banished them from the garden of Eden. He drove them out to work the ground and live out their lives away from His presence. No more would they walk together and talk to each other face-to-face. Think about how difficult it is for you when someone you are very close to dies. There is an ache in your heart, an emptiness that just cannot seem to be filled because the person who occupied that space is no longer here. You can never see that person face-to-face again on this earth. This is what happened when Adam sinned. He disobeyed God and gave away his authority to Satan because of that action, and now he was spiritually dead. In time his body would die also. It's just that the power of that holy fire that covered his body before he sinned was so strong on him that it took nearly a thousand years for the effects of the sin to overcome his flesh and cause it to die. Adam and Eve were now on their own. Adam had to go out into the world and work the land to get it to provide to him food for sustenance so he and his family could survive.

CHAPTER 5

A Plan

Previously I stated that God cast Adam out of His presence to protect him. Adam was now in a fallen state. There was another tree in the garden that was unique in its qualities. This tree was the Tree of Life. If Adam and Eve had taken fruit from that tree in the condition they were in, they would have lived in a state of separation from God forever. He did not want that to happen; these were His children. More importantly, they were the beginning of a countless multitude of children that He wanted to have around Him—a family that He could lavish His love and gifts upon. No, He had to prevent them from being eternally separated from Him, so He drove them out and put into motion the plan necessary to legally redeem them back to Himself. You see, He gave Adam full control of everything. When Adam committed treason and gave his allegiance to Satan by disobeying God, everything regarding this earth was legally transferred over to Satan. You can see this in the New Testament when Satan was tempting Jesus in Luke 4:5–6:

Then the devil, taking Him up on a high mountain, showed Him all the kingdoms of the world in a moment of time. And the devil said to Him, "All this authority I will give You, and their glory; for this has been delivered to me, and I give it to whomever I wish."

God could not legally take any of that back because it was now in Satan's possession. He was bound by His own righteousness to not act in a manner that would be wrong. No, He had to find a man from Adam's lineage who could rightfully take back the authority from Satan so humankind could be redeemed back to the Lord God. But it had to be a man without the sin of Adam in his blood. So began the steps that would be needed to reestablish a relationship with His children that had been taken away by trickery.

The effects of sin worked quickly in humankind. Eve was given two sons, Cain first, then Abel. Cain committed the first murder when he killed his brother in the field. He had to be banished as a wanderer because of his sin. Now, the first parents of humankind were once again alone. Like God the Father, they too experienced the pain of losing their children. In time Seth was born to them, and the lineage continued. It wasn't long till the Lord was grieved that He had made man on the earth and His heart filled with pain (Genesis 6:6). He was going to wipe humankind from the face of the earth. But there was someone who walked upright and blameless among the people that got the Lord's attention. That was Noah. It had gotten to the point where man's wickedness had become great, and his every thought was on evil all the time. If you have children who have strayed from your intended good and reject your guidance and love, you just might be in a position to begin to understand where God was with His children. He instructed Noah to build an ark to save a remnant of humanity and the animal kingdom that had been created. All else would perish in an epic flood in which no land would remain visible but be covered by no less than twenty feet of water (Genesis 7:20).

CHAPTER 6

One Who Believed

So life started over with just eight people and a handful of animals and birds to repopulate the earth. God kept looking for someone He could establish a deeper, stronger covenant with—someone He could bless with His love and goodness. He was looking for a man who would trust Him and walk upright before Him of his own free will. He found that man in Abram. God spoke to Abram in Genesis 12, telling him to leave his country, his people, and his father's household and go to a land that He would show him. This was a pretty tall order of trust for Abram. In his time, economics were based on herding flocks. The more family members there were, the more animals that could be cared for. It takes a number of people to keep the household safe and cared for, just as it takes a number of people to care for the animals and assure their safety. God stopped Abram and gave him a challenge. In

Genesis 12:1–3, God told him to leave all that he knew, but He also made a promise to him:

I will make you a great nation; I will bless you and make your name great; and you shall be a blessing. I will bless those who bless you, and I will curse him who curses you; and in you all the families of the earth shall be blessed.

To further take in the magnitude of this challenge, his wife Sarai was sixty-five and barren—no children. Abram was seventy-five years old and was being told to leave everything behind and trust that the Lord God would keep His word. Abram did just that; he left his father's household, packed up Sarai and their possessions, and headed for the land God said that He would show him. God made a promise to bless Abram beyond what he could comprehend for his obedience. At that moment a wonderful event occurred. One of God's children made a conscious decision to trust Him based solely on His Word. That was what He was after—an opportunity to reestablish a relationship with His estranged children. Abram accepted the offer and decided in his heart to trust God on that promise of love.

Now Abram wasn't perfect, but his willingness to trust and believe the Lord was counted to him as righteousness. This can be found in Genesis 15:6, Galatians 3:6, and Romans 4:3. God kept working with Abram, stretching his vision and ability to believe Him for greater things. First, He demonstrated that His promise of blessing was very real by making Abram wealthy in livestock, silver, and gold (Gen. 13:2). Abram had been obedient to the Lord, but it was time for some additional pruning of negative influences. Because his nephew Lot had traveled with him toward this Promised Land, he also experienced the effects that the blessing brought. Strife began to rise up between Abram's herdsmen and Lot's herdsmen. It was getting crowded in the land with all of those animals and people, and they began fussing at each other over finding adequate grazing fields for the flocks.

Abram said to Lot, "Let's not have any quarreling between us; you chose whichever direction you would like to go, and I will go the other way."

Abram understood that he was being blessed because of the promise that God had made to him. By letting Lot chose the land he wanted and taking the opposing direction, he was again placing his trust in God. Of course, Lot chose the better-looking land, but it was located down in the direction of Sodom and Gomorrah where great wickedness was being committed by the men who lived there. That decision ultimately led to the loss of everything he had except his two daughters.

Once Lot headed out toward his new home, God took Abram aside for some vision casting. In Genesis 13:14, God told Abram to look north, south, east, and west. Everything he could see was to belong to him and his offspring forever. He further said that He would make his offspring like the dust of the earth, so that if anyone could count the dust, then his offspring could be counted. What a challenge that was to Abram's ability to believe God. He was getting older, still didn't have any children, and here God was telling him that the generations of children that would belong to him would be so numerous that they would not be able to be counted.

Have there been times in your life when someone tried to lift your belief in yourself up? Maybe an older person who believed in you tried to get you to see that somewhere down the line, you were going to become something great because they saw that you were somebody special. The problem that so many of us go through is that there are seemingly thousands of people and circumstances that put us down and tell us that we cannot achieve that something special. Everywhere we turn, there is an obstacle standing in our path, preventing us from success. Sometimes the only way to overcome those obstacles is to remove ourselves from the presence of the people who are being so negative toward us. Most people don't want to see you succeed because it exposes their own shortcomings and failures. They will put lots of energy into preventing you from succeeding instead of putting that same energy into their own success. That is why God had to separate Abram from the negative influences around him. God wanted to get him alone so He could be the positive influence that would allow Abram to become the success God knew he could be. Now that Abram was standing alone, God invited him to walk the length and breadth of the land that was to be his. He encouraged him to take a stroll and take in with his senses all of the splendor that the Lord was giving to him.

How many of you have given a gift to a child and encouraged him or her to explore what that gift is all about? Maybe it was a new bicycle and the child wore him or herself out riding it up and down the neighborhood streets. Or perhaps you purchased a new home and you took your children there for the first time and shared with them what was now theirs. Maybe they ran with great enthusiasm throughout the entire house and yard, taking in every inch with unbridled excitement. Or perhaps they hesitated, standing in awe, unsure of the magnitude of what was before them, causing them to be unable to move. It was your heart that raced with emotions ahead of theirs as you planned for their happiness. You may have been just as excited, or perhaps even more so than they, in anticipation of seeing their faces when they took in what you had presented to them.

Our Father God has these same emotions as He prepares His gifts for us. We are made just like Him, so it stands to reason that He feels these things like we do. Yes, it is on a scale that we probably could not imagine, but then again, maybe not so big. We can imagine His love by looking at our children through loving eyes that were made like His. Our excitement rises with our children's if we allow ourselves to enter into that world of wondrous enchantment with them and explore everything again for the first time through their eyes. He created the universe and all that is in it.

I suppose that He could technically be uninterested in our puny little corner of that great expanse, but quite the opposite is true. He is keenly interested in every aspect of your life. Compare His preparation of the universe to a set of expecting parents. They take time in preparing the nursery where this infant they are waiting on will be living. Every color has to be just right, every piece of furniture in just the right place. Curtains and linens are arranged just so, soft toys are placed in their own little corners around the room to make it cozy and inviting. Mind you that the infant who will be occupying this room will barely be aware of any part of this environment for some number of months. Over the course of the next few years, this little copy of Mom and Dad will explore and discover little mysteries about that room that the parents may have long forgotten about. It doesn't matter that the child won't be aware of the care that went into preparing that room, but it matters greatly to the parents.

It is the same with God our Father. We have barely begun to discover the many mysteries about our universe, but as we do go about exploring, we find that everything is perfect. We can plan long-distance travels with spacecraft because the math is consistent. The heavens move in a predictable and orderly manner, which allows us to calculate where an object will be at a given point in the future. We can send a craft into the heavens on a journey that could conceivably take many years, yet we can know with confidence that on the expected date, it will rendezvous with its intended target. We look into the night sky with wonder at the magnificence of the starry host above us and dream that one day we will travel throughout those heavens. Here on our little planet, we may hike up the side of a mountain covered with dense forest, and as we come into a clearing that gives us a glimpse of the landscape below us, it takes your breath away. The absolute majestic beauty that stretches out before you is what God did for you. That is the effect that God was going for when He made all of this. It was done for us, no one else but His children. So yeah, we can imagine what it must be like for Him to watch us take in what He has given us with pure joy and amazement. We get to experience those same emotions and feelings with our little offspring.

Yes, there are what we call reality checks. Life steps up and kicks us in the shin in the shape of a three-year-old having a bad day. We may stop and reflect on the pressures that are being applied to our lives and wonder, is it really worth it? Am I doing the right thing, and does it matter to anyone else? It seems like I am working away at life day after day but not really getting anywhere except another day older, another day closer to death. It is a feeling that countless millions of people before us have also had. Abram had those moments too. He was feeling a bit of self-pity one day, and the Lord came to talk with him about it.

In the fifteenth chapter of Genesis, the word of the Lord came to Abram in a vision: "Do not be afraid, Abram. I am your shield, your exceedingly great reward." The Lord could see that Abram was having a bad day, and He came to cheer him up. He told him, "Don't be afraid, buddy. I've got your back. I won't let anything happen to you, and I will make sure that everything turns out great." But Abram was having his doubts. His response was, "Lord God, what will You give me, seeing I go childless, and the heir of my house is Eliezer of Damascus?" He had forgotten what God had told him about the dust of the earth representing the number of his descendants. God could see that Abram needed another confidence booster, another faith-building exercise.

How many of you have had a similar conversation with a youngster? They are trying to do something, but they are struggling with it. You can see the frustration in their demeanor. It is obvious to you that they are lacking confidence in themselves, and you stop what you are doing to help pick up their spirits. We are so much like our heavenly Father. It's remarkable that we don't see that in ourselves. The world has spent generation after generation removing God from our thinking. Man has tried repeatedly to elevate himself above God, saying to himself, "I have done this thing with none other but my own intellect and hands." Remember Satan, the fallen angel that wants to elevate himself above God? When humankind fell into sin because of Satan, he became our lord and master. In a sense, he became our spiritual father. Jesus points this out in the gospel of John 8:44 when He is talking to the Jews. He tells them:

> *You are of your father the devil, and the*
> *desires of your father you want to do. He was*
> *a murderer from the beginning, and does not*
> *stand in the truth, because there is no truth in*
> *him. When he speaks a lie, he speaks from his*

own resources, for he is a liar and the father of
it.

That is where we get it from, this desire to say and act like we don't need God. We can do anything we put our minds to, and nothing can stop us if we just keep at it—nothing except the fact that we are not in control of our circumstances and truly cannot do everything for ourselves.

That is why we are in the mess that we are right now. We are like that three-year-old toddler having a tantrum because things aren't going the way we want them to go. That is the fallen side of our humanity showing itself. But then there is the patient and loving parent who sees the toddler struggling and carefully takes the time to help and encourage that child. That is the side of humanity that is still connected to our Creator. His desire, God's desire, is to hold us when we are down, to sit down right next to us and talk with us. He wants to encourage us and help us to realize that it will be okay. Things will get better, and we can achieve those things that we were designed to do. We just have to be willing to lean on Him for His wisdom and guidance.

That is what Abram was going through. Here he was having conversations with the creator of the heavens, the one who told him that the number of his descendants would be as numerous as the dust grains on the earth. But Abram forgot about that revelation and was complaining.

> Then He brought him outside and said, "Look now toward heaven, and count the stars if you are able to number them." And He said to him, "So shall your descendants be." (Gen 15:5)

God gave Abram a way to refresh his spirit whenever he was down. All he had to do was pull back the door to his tent and look up into the night sky. The dream would come alive again in that moment when he was looking at the millions of stars that filled the night sky. When Abram looked into the sky at the moment that God took him outside, he believed God. He had no doubt in his heart whatsoever that God would fulfill what He had said. That is what thrills God. When you just believe Him and accept what He says as the truth and there is nothing that anyone else can do about it, He takes notice.

CHAPTER 7

Trust

Now to get to that point where you have such a firm foundation that you cannot be moved by the circumstances, you have to develop a strong relationship. This kind of trust and acceptance doesn't just happen on a whim; it takes commitment to build trust. A child who is growing under the guidance of a loving father spends time watching and imitating everything his father does. The loving father is careful to share only the truth with his son, even if sometimes it is painful. He is sure to back his every word with actions that secure the trust and confidence of his child. Over time, as a result of many conversations and questions and repeated lessons given, the child begins to develop a trust that what the father says, regardless of what he can see, is true. That is when a deep closeness begins to grow between the child and the father. The boy hears dad say something about a topic, and he just accepts it, no questions and no doubts. Dad said it, so it must be the truth, and that settles it. And the greater that relationship grows, the more the boy grows firm in that trust. Then when people say something contrary to what his dad said, or they tell him that his dad is wrong, then everything within him will rise up with strong conviction against the statement that is being made against his dad. That is the kind of relationship God wants with each of us. He wants you to grow so close to Him and have such a deep trust in Him that no matter what anyone says, you will stand with everything that is inside of you and say, "No, you are wrong. My God loves me and would never tell me a lie!"

Satan hates this love between God and man. He has been doing everything in his power to break this bond and get man to turn his back on God. Most everyone alive has been taught that God expects you to live up to standards that are impossible for us to meet. You may have been taught that He is an angry God who is waiting for you to mess up so He can punish you. In fact, you may have reached a point in your life where you thought to yourself, *Why bother? There is no way to meet the expectations of God, so why keep trying?* Just about every person I have talked with has admitted having these same feelings at one time or another during their lifetime. Some of us even lived that out by turning our backs on God. Why try to appease a vengeful God who just dishes out punishment by causing sickness, disease, and death? Why try to figure out a God who takes people you care about from you by allowing disasters or wars to kill them? Maybe you stood in defiance, shaking your fist as you shouted in anger back at Him. Maybe you cursed and called Him names as your heart was being torn in two from the loss. Maybe you spent night after night crying yourself to sleep, wondering what it was you did that made Him so angry at you that He brought this calamity upon you.

Whatever the situation was that caused you to blame God, the root of that was Satan. He took control of this world from Adam and hasn't stopped causing one disaster after another since. Worse than that, he studies each of us very closely to see what makes us tick. He is the most attentive student of human psychology there ever was. He works very diligently at making sure that you are hurting, and then he whispers in your mind that it is God's fault that this is happening to you. It is from within your mind that he attacks you and keeps you so focused on the problems that you cannot see the solution. His goal is to lie to you and cause you to not see that it is him causing you the pain and torment that is going on in your life. In John 8:44, Jesus said,

> *You are of your father the devil, and the desires of your father you want to do. He was a murderer from the beginning, and does not stand in the truth, because there is no truth in him. When he speaks a lie, he speaks from his own resources, for he is a liar and the father of it.*

Jesus was trying to teach people about His purpose on earth and they didn't receive His truth because they were only hearing the lies that Satan was telling them. Satan did not want them to realize the truth and be set free. God just wants to spend time with His children, but He is the one who is an outcast from the home He made for them. His heart aches for that closeness with each and every one of us. He continually tries to reach out to us through various means. It may be through His creation and the awesome beauty of it. You cannot help but see the fingerprints of God in nature. The closer you look, the more intricate the details are. While there are stories that say all of this happened by chance and over eons of time, the complexity of life has been evolving and changing. But when you really take in what is around you and ignore the lies that say God is dead or that He had nothing to do with all of this, you cannot help but see His handiwork. Have you ever had an opportunity to be up very early in the morning, before life wakes up? To be still before the world and listen to creation wake up from its slumber? It is an incredible event that is played out every day. I challenge you to do this tomorrow morning, regardless of where you are. Be outside an hour before sunrise and just take in the stars. Smell the air, and take in the scents of all of the plants, trees, and flowers around you. But most of all, stand still and listen closely to the silence. At first it is almost overwhelming. It is so quiet that it has a thickness about it that you could cut with a knife. Then it happens—a slight chirp from a tree over your shoulder, a whistle from somewhere ahead of you. They are soft and few at first, but before long, you begin to hear the choir warming up their voices. Every bird alive wakes up and sings their song, the one God gave them. If you listen, really listen, you can almost put words to the song and hear them celebrating life and thanking God for it.

Another way that God is trying to reach out to you is through that small, quiet voice that comes from somewhere deep down inside of you. Some people refer to it as their conscience that causes them to think twice about doing something wrong. It really is God and His effect on us because He made us. Hebrews 8:10 tells us that the Lord said He would put His laws into our minds and would write them onto our hearts. That small, still voice is God leading you toward a path of kindness and mercy. That is Him calling out to you because He wants you to know Him and that He loves you. But we need to make that effort to reach out to Him, to find out what He is really like and not listen to all of the lies we have been told or taught. It's the same as waiting for nature to wake up and listening close to the song they sing. If you listen close, you will hear the voice of God speaking softly to you. He will not speak harshly to you; He will not put you down or ridicule you. He only speaks in loving and encouraging tones to your heart. He knows that we are fragile creatures deep down inside. He uses gentle words to coax you out of your fearful shell that you are keeping out the harshness of the world by hiding in, so that He can show you the full depth of His love. He sees in us possibilities of great success and encourages us to step out and become the greatness that is within us. He will even change our names to reflect what we are to become rather than what we think we are. He did that with Abram

CHAPTER 8

Friend of God

Abram was ninety-nine years old and God appeared to him again. He saw in Abram the future of humanity and needed him to see that as well, so He changed his name. He told Abram that his name would now be Abraham, a father of many nations. He also changed his wife Sarai's name to Sarah, for she was to be a mother of nations. Kings of people would come from her. By changing their names, they had to refer to each other that way, and when they met new people, they introduced themselves as the father and mother of many nations. They began speaking what God saw in them. Their faith began to grow, and it had an effect on their bodies. These two old people started to change, and their bodies didn't act old anymore. In time Sarah's body became stronger and younger and was then able to conceive. God had made a promise to them and His word was sure, but He had to build that trust relationship with Abraham over time. That relationship began to have an effect on his physical body so that it became stronger, more vigorous and youthful. It took twenty-five years from when God first spoke to them before their bodies were ready to receive the promise that had been made to them, but they were finally able to receive that promise. It's like that child that over time develops the relationship with his dad so that deep down inside he knows that whatever his dad says, it will be so. That is what God did with Abraham. He took time to develop that trust with him, and Abraham believed to the point that whatever God said, regardless of how it may have sounded at the time, it would turn out all right.

God kept his promise to Abraham and Sarah and gave them a son. He was one hundred years old when Isaac was born. They called him Isaac, which means laughter. This boy brought great joy to his parents. God continued to bless Abraham, keeping the covenant promise that He had made with him. Isaac grew, and Abraham loved him greatly. Over the years, Abraham's faith had been growing. His trust in God was growing stronger, burning in him so brightly that the people of the land recognized that he was indeed blessed because of God. In Genesis 21:22, Abimelech stated, "God is with you in all that you do. Now therefore, swear to me by God that you will not deal falsely with me, with my offspring, or with my posterity." It was obvious to those around him that God truly was his shield and great reward, and they wanted to have Abraham on their side. When you walk with God and trust him as Abraham did, people take notice. Some will stay at a distance, somewhat fearful of you. Others will be drawn to you, curious of the blessing and its impact on your life. Abraham would not be influenced by those around him but only trusted God for his blessing.

He drew so close to God that God considered Abraham His friend, and when the time came that God had to dispense punishment out onto the cities of Sodom and Gomorrah, He stopped to discuss it with Abraham. The story is told in Genesis 18:17–18:

> *And the Lord said, "Shall I hide from Abraham what I am doing, since Abraham shall surely become a great and mighty nation, and all the nations of the earth shall be blessed in him?"*

Abraham had grown so close to God that the Lord God decided to discuss his affairs of dealing with man and his sinfulness with him before proceeding. Abraham understood the purity and righteousness of God very well. Because of his relationship with God, he interceded for those cities. God doesn't want any harm to come to anyone who doesn't deserve it. Abraham understood this and presented his case to God. He negotiated with God to obtain their deliverance. He asked God to spare the cities for the sake of righteous men within them. He went so far as to ask if there were only ten remaining, that God spare the cities for their sake. Now these were not small villages but cities teeming with people. Try to imagine this scene as it unfolded. Here is Abraham talking to the God of the universe, asking Him to be merciful on a region of the world in which the wickedness was so foul that He had determined they needed to be destroyed—destroyed so completely that the cities would never be rebuilt again. That can only be done because of a love relationship with trust so deep that the lesser can stand before the greater with confidence, knowing that his words will be heard without retribution. Not only that, but his words will be considered and have influence on the decision of whether or not to carry out the destruction.

This is the type of relationship that God the Father desires to have with each of us. He wants to have us discuss with Him our dreams and desires. He wants so very much to just sit with us and listen to us pour out our hearts to Him about every little thing that matters to us. He truly wants to discuss with you His plans. In Jeremiah 29:11, He says, "For I know the thoughts that I think toward you, says the Lord, thoughts of peace and not of evil, to give you a future and a hope." He wants to do this because it matters to Him. He has created heavenly beings, angels, to minister to us. In His Word, Psalm 91:11–12, it says, "For He shall give His angels charge over you, to keep you in all your ways. In their hands they shall bear you up, lest you dash your foot against a stone." He so desires to care for us that He commanded the angels to watch over us, to protect us from harm. But that care and protection are a result of a relationship with Him. If you don't know Him, if you don't have that closeness and trust between you and Him, how can you know and be confident that this care will be extended to you? It takes you making that step toward Him to find out what He desires for you. Think of a little child who is attempting to make decisions that could potentially be harmful to himself. He has a limited understanding of how things are around him and has limited abilities because of his size and strength. Now he could take pause and talk to his father about the things that he wants to do. His father has a great deal more wisdom and understanding and doesn't want any harm to come to his child. He would be willing to guide the son and help him grow into the venture he is contemplating. He would show the son what needs to be done now and what needs waiting on. He would show the son the path that would give him the greatest success. But if the son proceeds without asking for his father's guidance, the entire plan may be for naught. This same thing applies to the heavenly Father. You need only to ask and take the time to hear and understand His response.

Abraham's trust and belief in what God had told him was so strong that nothing would shake his relationship with Him. God had told him that through his son Isaac, He would have nations of people come from him and that all of the families of the earth would be blessed through him. God tested that faith. In Genesis 22:2, it is recorded:

> *Then He said, "Take now your son, your only*
> *son Isaac, whom you love, and go to the land*
> *of Moriah, and offer him there as a burnt*
> *offering on one of the mountains of which I*
> *shall tell you."*

That was no small request. God emphasized that he was to take his only son and specifically reminded him that this was the son that he loved. He told him to take him for a burnt sacrifice. Now Abraham had all night to think about this, to contemplate what God had told him to do. It is recorded that he got up early the next morning and saddled up his donkey, got a couple of his young servant men, chopped some wood for the fire, and took Isaac with him to the place where God had instructed him to go. Now Isaac was no small boy. Enough time had passed from his birth that he was most likely a young man himself. About the third day of their travel, they could see the place of their destination off in the distance. Abraham told the young men, "Stay here with the donkey; the lad and I will go yonder and worship, and we will come back to you."

He had been told to sacrifice his only son and set him on an altar and burn him in honor of his God, yet he told the young men, "We will come back to you."

Remember, the boy was now a young man. Abraham was well over the one hundred mark in age. When they arrived to the mount where God had directed them, Isaac asked his father where the lamb for the offering was. They had everything they needed for the sacrificial offering except for the animal. Abraham had been diligent about spending time with his son and developing that trust relationship. Isaac was very familiar with the elements of making an offering to the Lord, for he was with his father learning how all of this worked, what was done, and why it was done. Abraham responded to Isaac by saying in Genesis 22:8, "My son, God will provide for Himself the lamb for a burnt offering." After that, they went on to complete the task. Abraham built an altar, laid the wood on it, and then bound Isaac and laid him on the wood where the lamb should go. Abraham had built that trust relationship with his son, just as God had built that relationship with him. The young man didn't fight back but in obedience to his father, allowed him to bind him and place him on the altar.

Abraham's confidence in what God had said about Isaac being the future was so strong, so unshakable, that he figured God would raise Isaac back up from the ashes to keep His covenant promise. He went on in complete trust and obedience to God to finish his task. It is recorded in Genesis 22:11 that at the last moment, the angel of the Lord called to him from heaven and said, "Abraham, Abraham!" He stopped him and said, "Do not lay your hand on the lad, or do anything to him; for now, I know that you fear God, since you have not withheld your son, your only son, from Me." Hmm ... Sounds like shadows of things to come from the Father.

He had Abraham offer up a ram that was caught in a thicket on that altar instead of his son. This place was named after God. Abraham called it *The-Lord-will-provide*, after the name of God, Jehovah-Jireh. Then the angel of the Lord spoke again and said:

> *By Myself I have sworn, says the Lord, because you have done this thing, and have not withheld your son, your only son—Blessing I will bless you, and multiplying I will multiply your descendants as the stars of the heaven and as the sand which is on the seashore; and your*

descendants shall possess the gate of their enemies. In your seed all the nations of the earth shall be blessed, because you have obeyed My voice.

Remember when I pointed out that God had to put a plan into motion to legally establish a relationship with man and redeem him back to Himself? He had to get someone to, of their own accord, of their own will, step out in faith and believe what God said and act on it. Abraham did just that. He trusted God implicitly and was willing to take Him at His word and do it. This act of faith allowed God to now have that personal relationship with His creation, man, in the earth again. This set in motion what was needed for God to present His Son, His only Son, whom He loved very much, as a sacrificial offering.

CHAPTER 9

Rags to Riches

From Abraham came Isaac. From Isaac came Jacob and Esau. Jacob wrestled with an angel at Mahanaim, and the angel said that his name would no longer be Jacob, but Israel. From Israel came the twelve sons, which represent the twelve tribes of Israel. The families that trusted God were increasing as promised. Keep in mind that these were still men operating under the curse that was brought upon humankind by Adam, but they were being blessed because of Abraham. Within the family there was distrust, envy, and strife. Eventually the sons of Israel sold off one of their brothers, Joseph, to a caravan and told their father that he had been killed by wild animals. Satan is still the god of this world and is operating to prevent God's plan from working out. He is going to do everything he can to cause strife and hatred to grow between people, even between brothers.

The strife between Joseph and his brothers came about because Israel loved Joseph above the other brothers and of dreams that he had. In his dreams, there were sheaves of wheat, each representing one of the brothers, that bowed down to the sheaf that represented himself. He had another dream in which the sun, the moon, and eleven stars bowed down to him. This dream represented his father, mother, and brothers bowing down to him. God was foretelling the future by a dream to Joseph, but to his brothers, it was nothing more than Joseph lifting himself above them. They began to hate him and distanced themselves from him. When an opportunity presented itself to be rid of this pest, they took it. We still have the seed of evil within us, and when watered, it will produce awful results. Now the brothers agreed together to lie to their father, and it drove him into despair.

Joseph ended up a slave in Egypt. He didn't let the circumstances dictate his future though. Wherever he went, he trusted God and did only what was right by God's standards. Because of this, everything he did was blessed and prospered. He was first sold into the house of a man named Potiphar who was an officer of Pharaoh. Joseph did not rebel over his circumstances but rather kept his heart's focus on God. While in service to Potiphar, he did everything with excellence. Because his heart was trusting God, everything he did prospered. Potiphar took notice of this and elevated Joseph to overseer of his house and put him in authority over all that he had in his house. Joseph was likely just about twenty years of age but was now running the household of a respected officer of Pharaoh's kingdom. Joseph was a respected, talented, and handsome young man. Even the wife of Potiphar took notice of him. She approached Joseph and desired him to bed with her. Joseph would not let his integrity be compromised and even with repeated advances by her, he would not sleep with her. He informed her in Genesis 39:9, "How can I do this great wickedness, and sin against God?" Because he refused to do this, she turned on him and told her husband that he tried to rape her. Potiphar had him thrown into prison because of the accusation.

The covenant promise of God was still at work even in the dungeons of Egypt. Joseph kept his integrity intact even in prison. God had favor on him, and all that he did prospered. The keeper of the jail took notice and elevated Joseph to be in charge of all of the prisoners under the jailer's care. Even when things are going bad for us and it seems the world around us is caving in, God's desire is to stand right there with us and make sure we come out on top. Joseph held onto his dreams, and because he trusted God, he was able to interpret the meaning of other people's dreams correctly. Eventually, after many years, an occasion came about where Pharaoh had two dreams and none of his magicians could interpret the dreams. The dreams are described in Genesis 41. In the first dream, Pharaoh was standing by the river when out of the river came seven cows. They were fine-looking, fat, and healthy and began feeding in the meadow. Behind them came seven more cows from the river, but they were thin and sickly looking. They came up and stood by the other cows in the meadow. Suddenly, the sickly cows ate the fat, healthy cows, and at that, Pharaoh awoke from his dream. After falling back to sleep, he saw seven heads of grain form on a single stalk. They were plump and good heads of grain. Then he saw seven thin heads of grain sprout up on a stalk. These were dry and blighted because of the hot east wind. These seven blighted heads of grain consumed the healthy, plump heads of grain until they were no more. Pharaoh woke up and realized that these were dreams, but he did not understand them. They troubled him and he inquired of his council of magicians, but they were unable to decipher the dreams for him.

It was told to Pharaoh that Joseph could decipher the meaning, so he was called up out of the dungeons, cleaned up, and brought before Pharaoh. In Genesis 41:16, it is recorded, "So Joseph answered Pharaoh, saying, 'It is not in me; God will give Pharaoh an answer of peace.'" Joseph knew it was not of himself, but by God that these things would be made known. He was standing before the most powerful king in the land but gave all respect and trust to God. God gave him the meaning of the dreams, and Joseph explained them to Pharaoh. He told him that the dreams indicated that there were going to be seven years of plenty in the land. Abundant harvest would come from those seven years. After those seven years, there would be drought and famine in the land for seven years that would wipe out the abundance of the previous years of plenty. Furthermore, because the two dreams were one and the same but the message was repeated, this event was established and would definitely happen. Joseph told Pharaoh to select and appoint a wise and discerning man over Egypt to gather in the excess of abundant grain over the seven years of plenty and store it against the years of famine that were to come. Pharaoh said to Joseph in Genesis 41:39–40:

> *Inasmuch as God has shown you all this, there is no one as discerning and wise as you. You shall be over my house, and all my people shall be ruled according to your word; only in regard to the throne will I be greater than you.*

Pharaoh elevated Joseph to second in command of the entire kingdom. Only Pharaoh himself was above Joseph. He was elevated from the bottom to the top in a matter of two sentences. The blessing was again at work. This same blessing that God made as covenant promise to pour out on Abraham and his descendants was at work in Joseph. Some thirteen years had passed since Joseph was sold into slavery, but now he was in a position of power. At the age of thirty, he stood before Pharaoh and was placed into office, second in command. No one person could lift his hand or foot in the land of Egypt without his consent. It was because Joseph trusted in God that this took place. He used wisdom, given by God, to prepare the land for the coming famine that was foretold in Pharaoh's dreams. You see, God knew the famine was coming and used Joseph to protect the people to whom His promise had been made. Poverty, death, and destruction are the tools of Satan; abundance, life, and blessing are from God. God arranged to store the excess grain that would come over the next seven years through Joseph. When the famine came, Egypt was the only place where food could be found. Eventually, everyone around gave their gold, their livestock, their land, and themselves to Egypt to get food because the famine was so severe. This eventually brought all of Joseph's family back to him, where they were reunited. Pharaoh gave the land of Goshen, the best of the land, to Joseph's family as a place to live, and they prospered there. It is recorded that they grew and multiplied exceedingly in the land.

In the midst of tragedy and despair, God still continued to bless the descendants of Abraham. What looked like a family being torn apart from within itself was only a pattern within the tapestry that God was weaving that would preserve them and even bless them bountifully. In each generation, a person was found that sought after God, keeping the relationship alive. Joseph lived to be 110 years old. He stayed in Egypt and saw his family flourish and grow. In fact, they increased abundantly, multiplied, and grew exceedingly mighty, and the land was filled with them according to Exodus 1:7. When your relationship with God is good, He makes it very good.

God the Father really does want to make your life increase abundantly and make you and your family exceedingly mighty. Man, by way of Satan's influence, has tried to push Him out of our homes and our hearts ever since the fall from grace in the garden. But He won't give up. Like a father looking for a missing child, God the Father never gives up. There is an ache in the heart when a child that you love cannot be found. Nothing will stop you from searching every possible corner of the earth to find that child. He is the same way; nothing will stop His love from finding you. He just wants to put His big arms around you and hold you. He wants to show you that He loves you and that, if you will let Him, He will make everything all right.

Let's look at Psalm 23. This was a psalm written by David showing his confidence in God's grace.

The Lord is my shepherd; I shall not want.
He makes me to lie down in green pastures;
He leads me beside the still waters. He restores
my soul; He leads me in the paths of
righteousness for His name's sake. Yea,
though I walk through the valley of the shadow
of death, I will fear no evil; for You are with
me; Your rod and Your staff, they comfort me.
You prepare a table before me in the presence
of my enemies; You anoint my head with oil;
My cup runs over. Surely goodness and mercy
shall follow me all the days of my life; and I
will dwell in the house of the Lord forever.

Let's break down this Psalm so that you can see why David trusted God so much. "The Lord is my Shepherd; I shall not want." To understand this, we need to examine how the people of David's time understood farming and the care of animals. Goats and sheep were the main animals that were utilized. Goats had to be driven along by the shepherd using a stick, a driving rod, but sheep would follow their shepherd willingly. The shepherd of goats could be compared to Satan, who drives people along a way that is difficult. They are forced to go to places where they don't necessarily want to go. If they deviate from the path that they are being directed on, pain is inflicted upon them with the driving rod. They would graze on whatever plants were available as they were pushed along.

The shepherd of sheep would walk before the animals, leading them by going first. This person spent so much time with them that they knew the sound of his voice and recognized his appearance. They learned to trust him so that wherever he went, when he called, they would follow along without hesitation. Sheep depend upon the shepherd to keep them safe from harm, to provide food and water, and to care for them when they get hurt.

"He makes me to lie down in green pastures; He leads me beside the still waters. He restores my soul; He leads me in the paths of righteousness for His name's sake." They knew he was going to make sure that they had good grass to eat and fresh water to drink. Sheep prefer pastures that are lush and tender. Grasses that are more stiff or dry will cut their mouths and allow for parasites to invade. They are also fearful of fast-moving water and will not drink from it. They will go so far as to become dehydrated and succumb to the heat rather than drink from a brook of fast-moving water. They need waters that are calm and gentle flowing. They trust that he will lead them to these things.

> *Yea, though I walk through the valley of the shadow of death, I will fear no evil; for You are with me; Your rod and Your staff, they comfort me. You prepare a table before me in the presence of my enemies; You anoint my head with oil; My cup runs over. Surely goodness and mercy shall follow me all the days of my life; and I will dwell in the house of the Lord forever.*

Pasture land often is found in valleys where shadows from the hillsides provide hiding places for wolves, lions, or bears. The sheep so trust their shepherd that they will not be afraid of these places. They are protected from any harm by the shepherd and are able to walk right before them, enjoying the banquet of lush greens provided by him. They are able to eat without fear because he is watching over them, keeping them safe.

This is how David saw God the Father. He saw Him as a Good Shepherd. He knew that wherever he went, God was watching over him, keeping him safe. He knew that even though his enemies were hiding in the shadows, looking for an opportunity to attack, God was right there protecting him. This is exactly how the Father desires to be with you. He wants to lead you to safe places where you can be at rest instead of being fearful. He wants you to have all that you need and even make it so that you always have more than enough. He has your best interest in mind and wants so very much to protect you from the evil that is in this world. This is all because He loves you more than you can imagine and wants to spend time with you every waking moment of the day and stand guard over you while you sleep. Isn't that just how a natural father is with the children he has and loves? A good father who has a tender heart toward his children is driven to do good for them by the love he feels within himself. He gives them just what they need while making sure there is plenty available for when they need more. Just look in your own cupboards at home. You have available additional resources that are there so you can provide more than enough for your children, but you, as a wise parent, only give them what they need for that moment

CHAPTER 10

—— ❦ ——

A Deliverer

—— ❦ ——

When we last looked at the children of Israel, they were living in Goshen of Egypt, under the leadership of Joseph, whose integrity and trust in God brought peace and prosperity for the pharaoh of that day. He saw in Joseph the blessing of God at work and in turn, blessed Joseph's family with the best of the land. They multiplied and grew exceedingly great. In time Joseph, his brothers and all that were of that generation died. Eventually a new pharaoh took power that didn't know Joseph or realized all that he did to cause Egypt to become great. He looked around at all of the Israelite children who flourished in the land and in Exodus 1:9 said:

> *Look, the people of the children of Israel are more and mightier than we; come, let us deal shrewdly with them, lest they multiply, and it happen, in the event of war, that they also join*

our enemies and fight against us, and so go up
out of the land.

He was afraid of them. He recognized that they were blessed and saw them as potential enemies to his kingdom. Instead of embracing their God, he felt threatened by these people and so determined that he would turn on them and make slaves of them. The pharaoh that knew Joseph's family had been given the land of Goshen, which was a part of Egypt. Remember the famine that was so severe that everyone around sold all that they had to Egypt? So all the lands and even the crops that grew out of those lands belonged now to Egypt. This new pharaoh felt that the Israelite children had gone on long enough prospering in the land that had been given to them and turned on them, even though they previously had been granted the right to dwell there and live in peace. Once again, the people God was blessing and establishing a relationship with in the earth were threatened by Satan through people that he controlled. As far as he was concerned, this was his earth, and he wasn't going to let it go without a fight. And these Israelites were a threat to him because the rest of the world could see that they were being blessed by God. He had to put a stop to it.

Pharaoh made them slaves and put them to work building cities for him. He set taskmasters over them and afflicted them greatly. But the more they were afflicted, the more they multiplied and grew. The people of Egypt were in fear of the children of Israel to the point of dreading them. The pharaoh even went so far as to tell the midwives to kill the sons that were born to the women of Israel. The midwives feared God and did not obey the command of Pharaoh. Because of this, God dealt well with them, and the people continued to multiply and grow mighty. So now Pharaoh commanded his people to keep watch and every son that was born to the Israelites should be cast into the river, but they could keep the daughters alive. This is record of the first persecution that the Israelite people have had to go through over the course of their existence on the earth.

In the midst of this genocide that was underway, a little boy child was born. The mother kept him hidden for three months until she could no longer hide him. She decided to lean on the mercy of God concerning the life of the boy. She made a basket and waterproofed it with pitch, put the boy into it, and hid him in the reeds by the riverbank in the area where the daughter of Pharaoh would come down to bathe. The boy's sister stood off a way and watched to see what would happen. Pharaoh's daughter and her maid servants came down to the river, and she spotted the basket sitting in the water. She sent her maid to retrieve the basket and discovered the boy inside. The baby started crying, and she felt compassion in her heart for him. She looked him over and said, "This is one of the Hebrews' children." At that moment the boy's sister ran up and asked if she should go and call a nurse from the Hebrew women to take care of the child for her. Pharaohs daughter said go, so the girl brought the boy's mother. Pharaoh's daughter instructed her to nurse the child and she would pay her wages until he was old enough to be weaned. When he was old enough, she brought him back to Pharaoh's daughter, and he became her son from that day forward. She named him Moses because she drew him out of the water.

The mother trusted God to keep her son alive better than she felt she could do. God made it possible for her to see her son live and even continue to nurse him until he could be weaned as a little boy. Once again, God was at work preparing a way for the people that He had made a covenant with to be delivered from the evil of the world around them. This boy Moses spent the next years learning from the best that Egypt had to offer. He was no threat to the throne of Pharaoh because he was an adopted son of the daughter of Pharaoh, not a natural son of Pharaoh himself. So he could learn right alongside Pharaoh's other children, getting the best private education available. It is recorded in Acts 7:22, "And Moses was learned in all the wisdom of the Egyptians, and was mighty in words and deeds."

Moses grew up knowing that he was Hebrew, an Israelite, but also learned Egyptian customs and ways. During the time that he was being nursed, his family was teaching him the practices of the Israelites. He was learning that there was a God of Abraham and of his family's history. He was probably told the story of how he was saved from the command of the pharaoh to slay the newborn Hebrew boys and perhaps had been told that the God of Abraham had a divine plan for him. This is evident in Exodus 2:11–12:

> *Now it came to pass in those days, when Moses was grown, that he went out to his brethren and looked at their burdens. And he*

saw an Egyptian beating a Hebrew, one of his
brethren. So he looked this way and that way,
and when he saw no one, he killed the
Egyptian and hid him in the sand.

So the Bible demonstrates that he knew who his people were and that he had been adopted into the pharaoh's family. But it is obvious that he was troubled by their treatment and felt that he needed to act. While God did have a plan to use him to set the children of Israel free from the persecution, it was not through murder.

It didn't take long for the news to spread and reach the ears of Pharaoh. Moses had to flee, and it had to be far enough away that he wouldn't be found. He traveled on foot through the deserts of Sinai, around the Gulf of Aqaba to the land of Midian. This journey is approximately 250 miles of harsh terrain. Have you ever done something so wrong that it drove you to put as much distance as you possibly could between you and the people you wronged? We all have a sense that we run and hide when we do something that is not right and our hearts convict us of it. Ever notice how little children will hide from their parents when they do something they know they are not permitted to do?

They may not know why they did it, but at the moment they realize it, they immediately begin to cover it up or hide themselves from it and their parents. This goes all the way back to the initial fall of Adam and Eve. When they realized that they had done wrong, they hid themselves from God the Father. This same fear behavior exists within us to this day. The fear, the compulsion to do wrong, comes from Satan, the spiritual father who took over when Adam committed treason and disobeyed God the Father. So that DNA of character and behavior gets passed from generation to generation as a result of the curse that was put on humankind.

But God the Father does not give up on His children. His deep, abiding love drives Him on to pursue us and rescue us from this slavery we have fallen into. So even though Moses had messed up the plans by committing murder, God didn't give up on him. He watched over Moses as he traveled across the wilderness and reached Midian. He found himself at a well that belonged to the priest of Midian. This priest had seven daughters. They were the ones that tended the flocks for their father. This would normally be the task of the sons, but since he didn't have any, the daughters learned the trade from their father. The girls were out tending to the flocks and came to the well and drew water to give the flocks drink. Other shepherds came and drove them away, but here came Moses again, rescuing those who were being wronged. It is apparent that part of his character was to look out for those that were being mistreated. He just naturally stepped into the gap and protected those he perceived as being wronged. This character trait of his was valiant but needed some grooming and maturation. He had demonstrated that he was a protector, but he tended to act before thinking. So he stepped up, drove the other shepherds back, and helped to water the flocks of the daughters of the priest of Midian.

This action is significant because Moses learned some things growing up. Remember that the Israelites were primarily shepherd people. The Egyptians detested shepherds as evidenced in Genesis 46:34, where Joseph is instructing his brothers on how to answer the pharaoh about their occupation. He tells them, "That you shall say, 'Your servants' occupation has been with livestock from our youth even till now, both we and also our fathers,' that you may dwell in the land of Goshen; for every shepherd is an abomination to the Egyptians." Moses understood that his brethren were shepherds, but he grew up Egyptian, learning to detest this behavior. But his character to protect and serve was stronger than the prejudices he learned and he drew water for the flocks. Now Moses didn't know who the girls were. All he knew was that they had arrived first, had drawn water for their flocks, and were driven back by the other shepherds who had shown up. He took action because of his internal character, not any perceived gain that might be had.

The priest of Midian's name was Reuel (also referred to as Jethro). When the girls returned early, he inquired as to why, and they told him the story of what Moses had done. Reuel invited Moses to eat with them. Moses found himself content to stay with them, and Reuel gave him his daughter Zipporah to become his wife. So began the next part of his life's journey. He spent the first forty years of his life getting the finest education possible at the time. He had learned how to rule with a strong arm the Egyptian way. Now he was learning how to shepherd flocks. What a fall from power this was. So much for that divine plan of God to use him to deliver his people. Now he was working for his father-in-law, making him wealthy. But God wasn't finished with Moses. This was a time of quiet reflection. Being a shepherd requires patience, a quiet strength, and a keen eye. It was a time of learning how to serve, not be served. This went on for nearly forty years. During this time the king of Egypt died, but the bondage of the Israelites did not end with his death. God did not forget these people or His promises.

It may seem as though God has forgotten us. We go through times of adversity and pressures against us so overwhelming that we think He has decided to punish us with these trials and afflictions. It's as if He Himself threw us into a dungeon and gave all of hell permission to torture us. But that is not the case at all. It is our own poor decisions that have caused the circumstances we are in. If we are not actively engaged in conversation with God the Father, how could we possibly know what His advice or words of wisdom are for us? Think about it for a moment—don't most of us inquire of our parents to get their input about important decisions? If not our parents, then someone that we hold dear and trust to provide us with guidance? Well, God has all of the answers concerning our future. He knows all that will affect us and wants so very much to give us that guidance. He wants the very best for us. In Jeremiah 29:11 it says, "For I know the thoughts that I think toward you, says the Lord, thoughts of peace and not of evil, to give you a future and a hope." But if we don't ask for His guidance and help, He is unable to assist us. He is a gentleman and will not force Himself upon us. But if we ask sincerely from the heart, well, He will pour out His love on us with the intent to give us everything that is good to benefit us.

The children of Israel were feeling like they had been forgotten. They cried out to God for release from the bondage they were in. He heard them and intended to set them free. He had made a covenant with Abraham, with Isaac and Jacob, and would keep those promises. Moses was tending the flocks of Jethro, his father-in-law, and saw a bush that was burning yet not being consumed. He decided to investigate this sight and said, "I will now turn aside and see this great sight, why the bush does not burn." This is recorded in Exodus 3:3. It was time for God to reveal Himself to Moses. He called out to him from the bush saying, "Moses, Moses!" That will get your attention, to walk up to a bush that is on fire but not being burned up and hearing your name called out from within the bush!

It's at this point that God spelled out His plan for Moses. He informed him that it was His intention to deliver the Israelites out of the hand of the Egyptians and give them the land of the Canaanites, the Hittites, the Amorites, the Perizzites, the Hivites, and the Jebusites. Then He dropped the big reveal onto Moses and said in Exodus 3:10, "Come now, therefore, and I will send you to Pharaoh that you may bring My people, the children of Israel, out of Egypt." Now that was a lot to take in. He found himself talking to God out of a bush that was burning, and He told him that he was being sent to Pharaoh to have him release God's people!

CHAPTER 11

The Calling

Moses was nearly eighty years old and has blown what he thought was his opportunity to be able to have some influence in relieving the persecution of the Israelites long ago. He had accepted his new life working for his father-in-law and was raising a family on the backside of the desert near Horeb, the mountain of God. It was time to settle into the latter years of life and just coast into a life of ease and pass the torch onto his children. Now God showed up and gave him a new assignment, one that required him to go back to the scene of the crime.

Moses felt the need to discuss this with God. "Who am I that I should go to Pharaoh, and that I should bring the children of Israel out of Egypt?" He was feeling very insignificant and expressed that to God. Haven't we all done that? Haven't we had a desire to be something more and then when it was presented to us, we backed up and started coming up with reasons for why we could not do that very thing! At this point God assured Moses that He would be with him and even told him that when he had brought the people out of Egypt, they would serve Him right back here at this mountain where they were having this conversation. Moses persisted by asking, "Okay, so when I get there and tell them that You sent me, what should I tell them your name is?" They only knew Him as the God of their fathers. There was no personal attachment by a name that identified His character. So God responded, "I AM WHO I AM." And He said, "Thus you shall say to the children of Israel, 'I AM has sent me to you.'" Wow, He told Moses to refer to Him as one who always IS. His name tells us that He is in the past, He is in the present, and He is in the future. I AM is always in each moment no matter when it occurs.

God was now building trust with Moses. He spent some time telling him about the events that were about to occur. He revealed that the king of Egypt would not let them go, not even by a mighty hand, meaning even an army wouldn't change his mind, so He Himself would demonstrate His power and do wonders to prove to all of the people there in Egypt who He was. He even told Moses that the people of Israel would not leave Egypt empty-handed but would plunder them of their gold, silver, and clothing simply by asking for them. He gave Moses details about His plan. He didn't send him on his way in a complete mystery but shared intimate details with him about their success in leaving Egypt. Moses persisted with more doubts by asking, "But suppose they will not believe me or listen to my voice; suppose they say, 'The Lord has not appeared to you.'" The Lord took time to assure Moses. He demonstrated His power by showing Moses that his rod, or staff, could be changed to a serpent when he threw it on the ground. He had Moses place his hand inside his cloak and pulled it out full of leprosy, and placing it back once again, it came out clean as before. Last He instructed him that he would pour water from the river on the ground and it would become blood.

Moses responded with, "O my Lord, I am not eloquent, neither before nor since You have spoken to Your servant; but I am slow of speech and slow of tongue."

He was reminding the Lord that it had been forty years since he had spoken the Egyptian language and he would be slow in speaking to Pharaoh. The Lord reminded him by asking who made man's mouth. He said, "Now therefore, go, and I will be with your mouth and teach you what you shall say."

Moses kept throwing excuses out for not going because he felt inadequate. The Lord was getting angry with him because of his doubt and unbelief in what He was telling him. He told Moses that He would have Aaron the Levite, his brother, speak for him and would be sending him out to meet him. He let Moses know that He would teach both of them what to do and what to say when the time was right. Additionally, He told him to take his rod with which he would do the signs that the Lord told him to do and Aaron would be a mouth for him, and he himself would be as God to Pharaoh. God let him know that He would be with him so deeply, that when in Pharaoh's presence, he would seem as God to them.

This is the same relationship that the Father desires to have with you. God wants to walk with you so closely that others will see Him when they look at you. This closeness can cause people to react in some strange ways when you walk into a room. Some people will be drawn to you because they will sense the love and peace of God emanating from you. Others will steer clear of you because they will fear you. This is because of the spiritual enemy that lives within them is afraid of God, and that fear manifests itself in them physically so that they will run from you. Some may be angered by your presence but not really know why they are angry. Just know that whatever way people react, if you are truly walking in a deep relationship with God, He will protect you and give you the words you need to say, right at the moment they are needed, regardless of the situation. That is what He was conveying to Moses: "I will be so close with you that when the moment comes, they will not harm you because they will see Me in you." You don't need to memorize a script or be concerned that the words you choose are wrong. I will put them into your mouth right when they are needed.

Moses went and spoke to his father-in-law and asked to be released so that he could return to Egypt and see his brethren. Jethro told him to, "Go in Peace."

The Lord said to Moses, "Go, return to Egypt; for all the men who sought your life are dead."

Now Moses could make the journey, confident that the Lord was with him, that he didn't leave his father-in-law in a bind by departing, and that he could arrive without a bounty on his head. He was learning. Instead of being impulsive, he did things the correct way and could now travel in peace. He began his travels, taking his family with him. Along the way the Lord reminded him that he was to do the signs and wonders just as he had been told but Pharaoh would harden his heart and still not let the people go. He was saying to Moses, "Don't be surprised by his reaction. I am letting you know in advance that even as these signs are shown to him, he will still not change his mind and let the people go." He even told Moses in Exodus 4:22–23:

> Then you shall say to Pharaoh, "Thus says the Lord: 'Israel is My son, My firstborn. So I say to you, let My son go that he may serve Me. But if you refuse to let him go, indeed I will kill your son, your firstborn.'"

He let him know that there was nothing that He wasn't prepared to do to free His children.

Up to this point, the people of Israel knew of God as the God of their fathers, Abraham, Isaac, and Jacob. They didn't actually have any kind of a personal relationship with Him. They knew that the fathers had spoken to and had heard from Him. But they had not experienced the personal, one-on-one relationship that had occurred in their fathers' lives. They knew of Him but didn't *know* Him.

To better understand the events of the confrontation of Moses and Pharaoh, it is important to understand how the Egyptian people lived at that time. The people had many pagan deities that they recognized as having authority over various parts of the earth and sky. The pharaoh himself was recognized as a living god in human form over the people. He was not only their king but their god, in touch with the many other gods that ruled the land. This mind-set was ingrained into their culture so deeply that those ties, those relationships had to be broken so that the Egyptian people would realize that the God of the Israelites was far superior to their pagan gods, including their pharaoh. In Exodus 4:16 God told Moses that Aaron would speak for him to Pharaoh and that He would make Moses as God. God was preparing the way so that they could stand before Pharaoh as representatives of God, the I AM.

Remember, leaders are responsible for all who are under their authority. The decisions of the leader affect the entire land, from their people to their possessions. It is not God's intention that anyone should be punished or that they should die without fully knowing Him and having a relationship with Him. But if the leaders of a nation will not humble themselves before God and recognize His authority, then their stubbornness will cause a ripple effect of calamities to fall onto their subjects and the land. God's desire was to have Pharaoh recognize His sovereign authority over all the land, for him to repent and release the children of Israel. He and all of Egypt would have been blessed because of the covenant promise that He made to Abraham, Isaac, and Jacob. He had told them that anyone who blesses them would be blessed by God in return. God was trying to reach Pharaoh and the people of Egypt so that they could live and be blessed. This would require Pharaoh to turn from the idea that he was a living god with complete authority over everyone and everything under his rule. Instead of the people worshiping Pharaoh and multiple other gods, they would need to simply worship the one true God. That would take some demonstration of power to show them just how much more powerful God was than their beliefs in the many gods they worshiped.

In Exodus 5:1, Moses and Aaron went in and told Pharaoh, "Thus says the Lord God of Israel: 'Let My people go, that they may hold a feast to Me in the wilderness.'" Moses had just returned from a forty-year journey in which he achieved the high honor of becoming a shepherd of sheep. This was the very thing that stood as an abomination to the Egyptian people, as we saw in Genesis 46:34. Moses boldly walked into Pharaoh's court and declared a demand that he let the Israelite people go out of his land into the wilderness so that they could worship their God and hold a feast to Him. People were not permitted to enter Pharaoh's palace, much less his court, unless Pharaoh bid them come. And anyone who was so bold as to make a demand of Pharaoh was sure to lose his life immediately right there on the spot. This didn't happen to Moses or Aaron because the Lord God of Israel made Moses as God before Pharaoh and Aaron his spokesman, as written in Exodus 7:1. Pharaoh and all of Egypt understood the concept of a living deity, so

Moses was given respect as such. It was because of God that he could stand before Pharaoh repeatedly and declare his demands without fear. The hand of God was upon him, and he could not be touched by any mortal being.

Thus began the process of God demonstrating His authority over each and every god that Egypt worshiped. He started with the god of the Nile (and water) by turning every source of fresh water to blood. Through every plague that came upon Egypt, God was challenging Pharaoh himself and his authority. It was the people of Egypt who suffered, not the children of Israel. Each plague was focused solely on the people of Egypt and the pharaoh. Each time Moses entered into Pharaoh's court and demanded that the children of Israel be let go, it was God, challenging Pharaoh to recognize His superior authority and to submit to that authority. Pharaoh would not yield, and that brought additional plagues onto his people. Each plague demonstrated God's authority over another god within Egypt's mind. They were suffering so much that they begged Pharaoh to let them go out of the land because Egypt was being destroyed. It finally came down to the last plague. Moses had been told by God in Exodus

4:23 that even after all of the miracles demonstrated by God, Pharaoh would still refuse and it would cost him his firstborn son. The time had come, and Pharaoh would not yield. Moses warned him what would happen, and it did. Not only did Pharaoh lose his firstborn son, but all of Egypt lost their firstborn sons, and it extended to the firstborn of the livestock animals as well. Not one household in Egypt was spared.

This is the point in time where God instituted the ordinance of the Passover. In Exodus 12, the Lord instructed Moses and Aaron exactly how the families of Israel were to conduct themselves concerning this time. Each family was to take a lamb that had nothing wrong with it, no blemishes or deformities. They were to take that lamb and kill it at twilight and take some of the blood and put it on the two doorposts and the lintel (above the door). Exodus 12:12–14 the Lord says this of the Passover:

> *For I will pass through the land of Egypt on that night, and will strike all the firstborn in the land of Egypt, both man and beast; and against all the gods of Egypt I will execute judgment: I am the Lord. Now the blood shall be a sign for you on the houses where*

you are. And when I see the blood, I will pass
over you; and the plague shall not be on you to
destroy you when I strike the land of Egypt.
So this day shall be to you a memorial; and
you shall keep it as a feast to
the Lord throughout your generations. You
shall keep it as a feast by an everlasting
ordinance.

This was a shadow of things to come in which the blood of Jesus would be applied to the doorway of our hearts and keep us from the plague of eternal death.

God had also instructed Moses to speak to the people and have them ask of their Egyptian neighbors for clothing, articles of silver, and articles of gold. God granted the people of Israel favor in the sight of the Egyptians, and when they obeyed, they received all that they asked for. The Egyptians urged the people to hurry up and leave before they all ended up dead. In this manner, they plundered Egypt without lifting a sword because the Lord blessed them according to His covenant promise to His friend Abraham. Pharaoh finally let them go, and all of the people of Israel, their flocks of animals, and the mixed multitude of people that were also with them gathered all that they had and departed into the wilderness with God leading them as a pillar of cloud by day and a pillar of fire by night.

Four hundred and thirty years had passed since Israel came to live in Egypt. To the day exactly, they left Egypt. The Lord God had told Abraham in Genesis 15:13 that his descendants would be servants in a strange land that was not their own for four hundred years. He also told him that they would come out of that land with great possessions. God kept His promise and released them just as He said He would. He even led the way out of Egypt. He stood before them as a cloud by day and as a pillar of fire by night. When you live in the desert, you deal with extremes. It can be incredibly hot during the day with the sun blazing down on you without a cloud in the sky to provide any relief. At night it can get very cold because there is nothing to keep the heat against the earth. The cloudless atmosphere just lets the heat escape, and the ground does not hold onto any of the warmth because it is arid sand. Once again, the Lord God was caring for His people. He led them along, both day and night, providing them a measure of shade against the hot sun via the cloud and warmth against the cold night via the pillar of fire. And since they had to leave in a big hurry, they didn't have time to gather up firewood or oil for lamps to provide them with light to see with in the night, God Himself provided that light.

CHAPTER 12

—⋯⋯ ∞ ⋯⋯—

Deliverance

—⋯⋯ ∞ ⋯⋯—

He led them through the wilderness until they arrived at the edge of the Red Sea. The Lord spoke to Moses and told him He was going to provoke Pharaoh one more time so he would bring his entire army to attack the Israelites. In Exodus 14:4 it states, "Then I will harden Pharaoh's heart, so that he will pursue them; and I will gain honor over Pharaoh and over all his army, that the Egyptians may know that I am the Lord." It was because of Pharaoh's stubbornness to submit to the Lord's authority that they would suffer a great loss. Pharaoh and his army came out after the Israelites, and when they saw the army coming after them, they cried out to Moses. They had witnessed the hand of the Lord against Egypt and had been set free with heaps of treasure piled onto them, yet now they were in panic. They focused on the size of the enemy coming after them instead of the size of the Lord who had rescued them. In verse 13 Moses said to the people, "Do not be afraid. Stand still, and see the salvation of the Lord, which He will accomplish for you today. For the Egyptians whom you see today, you shall see again no more forever."

The Lord God said that He would take care of this people and would be their great shield in times of trouble. If you are a parent and someone threatens to harm your child, everything within you rises up to protect that child from any harm. You will stand between the attacker and your baby and do your absolute best to whip that beast so they turn and run and will not come back to try that again. That is exactly what God the Father wants to do for you. He will stand between you and your enemy and cover you with His shield of protection. Psalm 46:1 says, "God is our refuge and strength, a very present help in trouble." Psalm 91 is all about the protection of God over us. It tells us that God will cover you with His feathers, and under His wings you shall take refuge. A mama hen will call to her chicks when she detects danger, and the chicks will run and gather themselves under her wings so they are protected. This is the image to put into your mind when reading that part of the Psalm. A hawk flying overhead cannot see the chicks because they are hiding under the hen, fully protected. If you will let Him, He will protect you too.

The Lord God instructed Moses to lift up his rod (staff) and stretch out his hand over the sea and divide it. When he did, the Lord caused a strong east wind to blow all night, which separated the waters of the sea and dried the ground. The people went into the midst of the sea on dry ground with a wall of water on each side of them. When the Egyptians pursued them on their chariots, the Lord looked down on them and caused the wheels to come off of the chariots and made it so they could not drive the chariots across the land. The soldiers realized that the Lord was fighting for the Israelites and attempted to flee, but the Lord instructed Moses, who was now safely on the other side of the sea with all of the Israelite people, to stretch out his hand once again and cause the waters to come back upon the Egyptians. When he did this, the water completely covered every one of the Egyptian army members so that none survived.

The only thing required of the people of Israel was to obey. The Lord God did all of the work and thus made His name famous in all of the lands around the region. Egypt's pharaoh was beaten. His land, the people, and the crops were in ruin. He no longer had an army to defend them, and the Israelites had plundered their riches and were now on the other side of the Red Sea. All of this destruction was a result of his arrogance and pride. He thought he was above God, and because he would not humble himself, everyone who was under his rule suffered. This is pretty much the same thing that happened to Lucifer, who fell into destruction because he thought he was above God. He and all he was responsible for were cast down out of heaven, and Lucifer became Satan and his fate was sealed. He knows that his time is limited before he is put away for all eternity, so his goal is to get as many of God's creation, humankind, to abdicate and follow him instead of God the Father. Many other leaders of nations throughout history have done the same thing, only to be overthrown and destroyed. The most wicked and despicable have virtually disappeared from history except for archeological remains that tell of their existence. The most recent attempt to eradicate God's chosen people resulted in a war that engulfed nearly every modern society of the globe and saw over sixty million people die. Approximately six million Jews were killed during the rampage of Adolf Hitler's Nazi regime.

But, in spite of this horrific tragedy, God's people prevailed. In fact, in May of 1948, Israel once again had its national borders defined and became a free state again. So from the ashes of these atrocities, Israel once again returned to a land that had been promised by God Himself. Over the ensuing decades, Jews from around the world have been making their way back to their homeland. The Jewish people, the Hebrews, have been considered God's children since the days of Abraham. This Father that the world calls God has been upholding His promises in spite of His disobedient children not always following through on what He has set down as what is necessary for them to be blessed and prosper. He made sure that they understood and had information written down to guide them through the ages toward success. But even as our own children get similar guidance from us as natural parents, the child doesn't always listen and follow through with obedience and sometimes need some form of correction to be applied.

Just as the people of Israel, the modern Jews, were saved from the hands of tyrants who were bent on their destruction, so were the children of Israel saved from the hands of the Egyptians. God Himself did the work in the rescue of Israel from Egypt to establish His name in the earth. All of the people who witnessed the awesome power of the Lord feared or reverenced Him. Ah, but there was much work to be done now. They had been freed from their captivity, from the burdens of slavery, but now all that they had known for many years and generations was gone. They were a free people in a land they knew nothing about. They absolutely had to trust the God of Abraham, the great I AM, for everything. This would take some time, and they would be tested again and again. They had to learn how to become a nation of people that governed themselves. They had many generations of having someone else telling them what to do as slaves, and now they were free. Sudden freedom from tyranny can cause reckless decisions to be made the moment pressure is applied. They needed to learn how to depend upon God, who loved them, but all that they had known is to depend upon a people who treated them with cruelty and hatred. They knew how to respond to that, but how to depend upon and respond to love was not something they had the knowledge to do.

There are various estimates of how many people left Egypt, and they range from two million to as many as six million. This number included the many non-Israelite people, who were not Egyptian but were relegated to the same slavery treatment and had left along with the Israelites. Plus, they left with all of their cattle, sheep, and goats. The first problem that a group of living creatures of this number would experience is thirst. All life depends on water. Days can go by without food, but beyond three days without water and death is close by. This multitude found themselves in that situation. They were only three days into the Wilderness of Shur, and they had not found water. The Lord provided them water, and He said to them in Exodus 15:26, "If you diligently heed the voice of the Lord your God and do what is right in His sight, give ear to His commandments and keep all His statues, I will put none of the diseases on you which I have brought on the Egyptians. For I am the Lord who heals you." He provided them with water and a promise to continue to care for them. Sickness and disease are another issue when you have that many people living together in a wilderness setting. They no longer had the structured routine for personal care that was afforded to them in Egypt. In order to survive, they were going to have to listen to what the Lord said so they wouldn't get sick.

Some forty-five days had gone by since they had left Egypt, as recorded in Exodus 16:1. Now the issue of food was becoming a problem. They began complaining to Moses and Aaron about what they remembered of the food that was around them in Egypt. Moses brought this before the Lord, and God the Father told them that He Himself would provide food for them. He told them that bread from heaven would be made available to them each day, but there were rules about this bread. They were to only gather a certain amount for each person and no more than that. It would only be available during the early morning to gather. Once the heat of the sun hit the bread, it would melt away and no longer be there. Last, this would happen for six days. On the sixth day they were to gather twice as much because on the seventh day there would not be any bread. This seventh day was the Sabbath, and they were not to work but use it as a day to worship the Lord God of Israel.

In Exodus 16:14–15, it records the beginning of this miracle of food from heaven:

And when the layer of dew lifted, there, on the surface of the wilderness, was a small round substance, as fine as frost on the ground. So when the children of Israel saw it, they said to one another, "What is it?" For they did not know what it was. And Moses said to them, "This is the bread which the Lord has given you to eat."

There were some who gathered more and hid a portion aside for the next day. When they went to make use of it the next morning, it had bred worms and stank. It wasn't fit for consumption. However, when the sixth day came and they collected twice as much, the portion that they kept for the Sabbath day did not have worms, nor did it stink. As long as they were obedient, the bread fed them just as the Lord said. The bread would show up every morning for six days, but not on the seventh. God would suspend the laws of physics every seven days so that the extra portion of bread that had been gathered on the sixth day was preserved for that Sabbath day. This continued for forty years while the people of Israel were in the wilderness until they came to the border of the land of Canaan.

A father who dearly loves his children has a desire within him to give his children the best that he can obtain. His heart has compassion for them when they are not doing as well as he thinks that they should be. He looks on them when they are struggling with problems and does what he can to guide them and help them overcome whatever the problem is. He does what is within his power to make sure that there are supplies in the cupboards so that when they are hungry there is food enough to prepare a meal for them. It may be Momma who does the cooking, but it is his heart that drives him to go out into the world and make sure that there is a way to obtain that food. This tender love comes from our heavenly Father. He has planted this into our hearts to be like Him. This love began with Him, and because we are made like Him, we have that same desire to give the very best to our children.

The Father God wanted to spend time, real up-close and personal time, with His children. He set them free, He made sure that they had water and food, but these are just basics for living. He wanted to be right in the middle of them every day so they could connect with Him, talk with Him, and have a personal relationship with Him. Just like a family that isn't quite complete unless Daddy is home with the rest of them, God knew that in order to make His family complete, He needed to be in the middle of their lives with them every day. He wants to be in the middle of your life too. He wants you to know Him so well that you won't make a move without giving thought to Him. He has a desire to bless you with all He has to make your life complete. He wants to hear you talk with Him, not just your prayers that you speak about your needs, but the personal conversations. We all spend time having very intimate conversations with the one person that we love dearly. We take time to listen to what the person is saying, and in turn we say what is in our hearts to share our deepest desires with him or her. That is exactly what God desires to have with you. He wants to talk with you in such a manner that you are sharing your deepest thoughts with Him, and in turn, He wants to share His deepest thoughts and desires with you. Most people spend their lives talking at God but walk away after they have their say without ever listening to see if God has something to say them. He wants to talk with you, not at you. That is what a conversation is, two people sharing and exchanging thoughts, ideas, and feelings.

Picture elderly grandparents sitting with a young child on their laps. The ones who truly love and cherish the grandchild will sit and listen to every word that comes out of that child's mouth. They will respond in a manner so the child understands what they feel and think by making their conversation plain and simple so that it is at the child's level of understanding. It is usually the child doing most of the talking, but the grandparent will encourage the child to tell all he or she has in his or her heart, and they sit with great attention to what the child has to say. As the child grows and this relationship develops into a close and intimate bond, the grandparent will find occasion to share more thoughts of wisdom and guidance with the child. It is the closeness of the relationship, the growing of that trust and love, that brings the child to begin to not only ask of the grandparent but to patiently listen and consider what is being said. It is the growth of the relationship, the maturing of the love and trust, that the child has for the grandparent that makes this happen. The Father God that we have desires to have this same level of relationship with you. He wants to hear your heart being poured out to Him. He wants to hear your hopes, your dreams, your passionate desires, and everything else you have to say.

110

He wants to develop a relationship of trust and love so you will pause and listen to see what He has to say about your hopes and dreams. This is because He wants to guide you with wisdom and gentle love so you can fulfill your future with great success.

It is with this desire in mind that God spoke with Moses and gave him instructions for preparing the children of Israel for having God come into their midst. In Exodus 19 He tells Moses that He wants the people to be His special treasure above all people. He wants them to prepare themselves for His visit. He tells Moses that He will come to them in a thick cloud, that the people may hear His voice when He speaks with Moses and believe him forever. He wanted to be in the middle of their camp. He wanted to be with them day and night and no longer be separated from His children. They got themselves cleaned up and ready for this special guest to come into their camp. The morning of the visit the top of the mountain had thundering, lightning, and a thick cloud over it. A trumpet sounded very loud to announce the coming of God to the mountain. The Lord descended onto the mountain in a cloud of smoke and fire, and the mountain shook with His presence. Then the trumpet blast sounded long and became louder and louder. With that Moses spoke, and God answered him by His voice. He called Moses up to the top of the mountain, and there He gave Moses what we now know as the Ten Commandments. Moses returned to the people and spoke to them about what God had given to him.

After he spoke the commandments that he received to the people, they made a statement that would define their future in a way that would hurt them more than they could possibly realize. Because the presence of the Lord was so powerful that the earth literally shook, they were very afraid. They told Moses in Exodus 20:19, "You speak with us, and we will hear; but let not God speak with us, lest we die." Because of their fear, they rejected God from being in their midst. He wanted to be able to talk with them and have them talk with Him, the same way He and Moses had conversation with each other. We still do this exact thing today. God wants to be with us in everything that we do, but we get afraid and tell Him to go away. Even though He is the source of all life and blessing, we let fear tell us that He is too much for us to handle. We lash out at the One who loves us and wants to help us. We even do that with the people who love us and want to help us. This is what fear does to people; it causes them to reject love and instead, spend time becoming intimate with grief and pain. Don't be like the Israelites and reject God. Let His love comfort your heart, and let yourself get to know Him. Satan wants you to fear the Father God, because then you won't get to know just how much He loves you and wants you to have every good thing so you are blessed.

This rejection didn't deter God in the least. He didn't go off and pout and boo hoo because His children didn't want Him to be with them. He is very determined that He will restore the relationship with His creation and He will succeed. His pure love, which is His very nature, will overcome the damage caused by Adam's rejection. To further demonstrate His love, in Exodus 24, He instructed Moses to have Aaron, Nadab, and Abihu and seventy of the elders of Israel to come up onto the mountain. Prior to them coming up to spend time with the Lord, Moses guided them in making burnt offerings and peace offerings to the Lord. Half of the blood from the animals was put in basins, and the other half was sprinkled on the altar. He had been instructed by the Lord to write a book of the covenant, and after these offerings, he read the book to the people. The people responded when he was finished by saying, "All that the Lord has said we will do, and be obedient." Moses then took the blood that was in the basins from the sacrifices, sprinkled it on the people, and said, "This is the blood of the covenant which the Lord has made with you according to all these words." With these actions, the people were sanctified. The blood was symbolic to covering their trespasses and sins. An innocent animal was sacrificed in their place, and they were now covered by that blood. These seventy-three people that the Lord had invited up to the mountain were sanctified by this action. Sanctified means set apart, made holy.

These are a part of the same people who had rejected God and told Moses they didn't want God to speak to them or they would die. Now they were standing on the mountain and in Exodus 24:10, they saw the God of Israel. They were standing in His presence, and they didn't die! People have been taught that nobody can stand in the presence of God and live, yet here is proof in the Bible that there were seventy-three people standing in front of God and lived. In fact, He served them dinner. It says in verse 11 that they ate and drank. God was standing on a sapphire stone that was so clear that it was like the heavens. He prepared a dinner for them and stood in their presence while they ate dinner. God the Father just wants to have dinner with His children and listen to their stories.

Isn't that what happens when families get together and have a big meal? Anyone who has been part of a family reunion has witnessed this happen. People who haven't seen each other for a time all come together, and it seems that it's always over a meal. I don't think there has been a family reunion that hasn't had a meal in the middle of it. People are naturally drawn to setting a table of food out and gathering around it so they can eat and talk and tell stories about their lives to each other. This is what is at the very heart of God to do with us. He sincerely desires to have all of His children gathered around him while He serves them a meal and gets to listen to all of the conversations going on between everyone. In fact, if you look at Revelation 19:6–9, the Scripture talks about the marriage supper of the Lamb. This is the wedding feast of the church (the bride) and the Lamb (Jesus, the groom), and God the Father puts on this feast so that all of His children are now gathered together in His presence having dinner. This is the ultimate end goal of God in reuniting Himself with His children: a magnificent family reunion over a magnificent meal where He can just be right there in the middle of the whole thing.

CHAPTER 13

The Redeemer

God has made great strides in reestablishing His relationship with His children. The people of Israel have seen His deliverance, His miracles, and His awesome power. Now He was showing them His love, His care and desire to be with them. But in order to truly be with them, He needed to make sure they sanctified themselves before they came into His presence. He did not want any harm come to them because of the sinful nature within them. The curse from when Adam disobeyed was still upon them. A temporary covering could be made through the sacrifice of an innocent animal, but it was only temporary. This sin still separated God from His family. But now He had established a covenant with a portion of humanity, and He told them that He would bless all nations through them. He was foretelling of a time when every person on the earth could have that personal relationship with Him, not just this select group of people. His plan was moving forward, and it would be through a descendant of Abraham. But yet, the curse was working through humankind. So this deliverance had to be a man, but a man without sin—someone who could pay the price necessary to redeem humankind back to God. Someone had to pay with his life by shedding his blood in place of the innocent animals. This price had to be so high and so pure that it would not just cover the sin, but completely remove it.

In Numbers 24:17, a man named Balaam made a prophecy about this man who was to come and set humankind free. It says, "I see Him, but not now; I behold Him, but not near; a Star shall come out of Jacob; a Scepter shall rise out of Israel, and batter the brow of Moab, and destroy all the sons of tumult." In Genesis 49:10, a similar prophecy is made: "The scepter shall not depart from Judah, nor a lawgiver from between his feet, until Shiloh comes; and to Him shall be the obedience of the people." The reference to a star, a scepter, and Shiloh all refer to the Messiah, Jesus. It is Jesus who had to come as a man and shed His blood in place of the innocent animals.

God continued working with His people, the Israelites. They had their tests and trials, their ups and downs, their failings and successes. Eventually they took possession of a land that God had promised long ago to Abraham. They were learning how to be a nation established by God, living separated lives different than those of the nations around them. God would use them as a light in a dark world to show all of His glory. The nation of Israel grew to power and dominance in the region, but they began to forget how they got there. They allowed their relationship to slip and let their love for God fade. This is the same thing that happens to so many marriages in our world today. For various reasons, the once-successful marriage begins to falter and weaken. The love begins to fade because they forget the vows they made to each other. God didn't forget His vows; He didn't forget His covenant promise to them. But because they would no longer listen, the very things that God had warned would happen to them began to overtake them. Eventually Israel lost their sovereignty and their land. They were taken captive, their land was left in ruin, and many were lost to the sword, famine, or pestilence. Eventually they were able to return to their land, but again other empires ruled over them.

Back in Genesis 3:15, God said, "And I will put enmity between you and the woman, and between your seed and her Seed; He shall bruise your head, and you shall bruise His heel." This was God foretelling of One who would come and over throw Satan and his authority in the earth. When God was establishing His relationship with Abraham, He tested his trust by asking him to sacrifice his son Isaac. Abraham so believed God was true to His word and was going to make his descendants as numerous as the stars that he willingly went up to the mount and put Isaac on the altar. At the last moment God stopped him and provided a ram to put in Isaac's place. Because Abraham was willing to sacrifice his son before God, because of the blood covenant between God and Abraham, it was God's obligation to be willing to do the same. The time had come for God to fulfill that obligation.

Over the millennia, there were many prophecies, foretellings, of a Messiah, the Christ, the Anointed One, the Savior of the world. These were provided by many different people inspired by the Spirit of God over many hundreds of years. One of those was a prophet named Isaiah. Here are some of the things that he foretold about Jesus. Isaiah 7:14, he writes that He would be born of a virgin. "Therefore, the Lord Himself will give you a sign: Behold, the virgin shall conceive and bear a Son, and shall call His name Immanuel." In 9:2, he tells of His ministry in Galilee: "The people who walked in darkness have seen a great light; those who dwelt in the land of the shadow of death, upon them a light has shined." In verse 7 of the same chapter, he tells us that He would be the heir to the throne of David:

> Of the increase of His government and peace
> there will be no end, upon the throne of David
> and over His kingdom, to order it and
> establish it with judgment and justice from
> that time forward, even forever. The zeal of
> the Lord of hosts will perform this.

In chapter 11 of his writings, he described some of His characteristics. Verse 2 says:

> The Spirit of the Lord shall rest upon Him,
> the Spirit of wisdom and understanding, the
> Spirit of counsel and might, the Spirit of
> knowledge and of the fear of the Lord.

He tells us that He is our only Savior and because of the price He paid, we are set free in 53:5: "But He was wounded for our transgressions, He was bruised for our iniquities; The chastisement for our peace was upon Him, and by His stripes we are healed." The stripes refer to the lashings that tore open His back by the scourging given by Rome before His crucifixion.

These various prophecies were written down and woven into Israel's history, even when they just didn't make any sense. Some two thousand years ago when Israel was once again being occupied by an empire, it was time for these numerous prophecies to come to pass. The prophets had foretold of the Messiah coming and being born among the people. They said that He would deliver God's people and establish His kingdom forever, without end. There would be signs in the heavens that would declare His birth, and He would be God with us, Immanuel.

The book of Luke tells us the story of this Christ. The angel Gabriel was sent by God to visit a young virgin by the name of Mary. He greeted her and said:

Do not be afraid, Mary, for you have found favor with God. And behold, you will conceive in your womb and bring forth a Son, and shall call His name Jesus. He will be great, and will be called the Son of the Highest; and the Lord God will give Him the throne of His father David. And He will reign over the house of Jacob forever, and of His kingdom there will be no end.

She didn't know how this would be since she was a virgin, so the angel answered her, saying, "The Holy Spirit will come upon you, and the power of the Highest will overshadow you; therefore, also, that Holy One who is to be born will be called the Son of God." This was how God was going to deliver humankind. His Son, His only Son, would be sent to be sacrificed to pay the price required of man. He would be a man, born of a woman but yet not from a man but from God Himself. God was going to fulfill His part of that covenant He made with Abraham. Abraham was willing to give his only son, and now God was willing to give His only Son.

This child grew as a boy within His Jewish community, learning all of the laws of Moses and His

Jewish history. He grew into a man, yet He didn't sin. He walked as a man but was very aware within Himself who His true Father was. At the age of thirty, He came to be baptized by John the Baptist and began His ministry. For three years He preached of His Father's love. Everywhere He went He healed the people, delivered them from demons, and restored both their bodies and their minds. This man showed up from seemingly nowhere and literally shook the entire world with His words. The region from which He traveled to deliver His message covered an area of approximately forty by eighty miles. He traveled mostly by foot or by boat to cross Lake Gannesaret (the Sea of Galilee). His family profession was that of a builder, a worker of wood and stone. He was referred to as a carpenter from Nazareth. He wasn't a man of any great fame or wealth, yet everyone that heard Him speak listened to what He had to say. His words seemed to pierce right through to the very hearts of those who heard Him. No one person before or after Him can measure up to the truth and wisdom that came from His speaking. He seemed to be able to speak with a clarity that no one could match. Yet, with all of this He was rejected by His family, declared a nut, someone who had lost His mind. In Mark 3:21 His family tried to lay hold of Him, saying, "He is out of His mind."

The religious rulers of the time were of the same opinion. Members of the religious council followed Him to each and every place He went, observing all He said and did. He called out their hypocrisy and challenged their unreasonable traditions. The more He preached, the more they grew to despise Him. Ultimately, they plotted on how to get Him killed. Even His disciples who were with Him day and night questioned His actions. But at their own admission, in John 6:68 Peter answered Him, "Lord, to whom shall we go? You have the words of eternal life." This man, this Son of God, was sent to set the captives free, to preach the gospel to the poor, to heal the brokenhearted. He was fulfilling the prophecy given by Isaiah in the sixty-first chapter, which He quoted in Luke 4:18–19:

> *The Spirit of the Lord is upon Me, because He has anointed Me to preach the gospel to the poor; He has sent Me to heal the brokenhearted, to proclaim liberty to the captives and recovery of sight to the blind, to set at liberty those who are*

oppressed; to proclaim the acceptable year of the Lord.

He counted Himself equal with God, and that enraged people. Many times they wanted to kill Him but were unable to. He called Himself the Son of Man, recognizing that He was descendent of Adam, yet He was also Son of God. He was God with us, yet people were still rejecting Him. He came to pour out His love upon us, and nobody wanted it.

Remember Isaac, Abraham's son? When Abraham took Isaac up to the mount to sacrifice to the Lord God, Isaac was a young man. He was old enough to whip Abraham if he wanted to. When Abraham began to bind Isaac and place him onto the altar, he could have resisted and fought back, but he didn't. He was obedient to his father and trusted him that what he was doing was good and his life would be restored by God. When it came time for Jesus to be crucified, He prayed to His Father about it. Matthew records in chapter 26, beginning with verse 39, that Jesus asked His Father, "O My Father, if it is possible, let this cup pass from Me; nevertheless, not as I will, but as You will." He was the Son of God, but He had to be willing as the Son of Man to allow Himself to be crucified in order to redeem humankind. The man was weak and didn't want to willingly give His life, but the Spirit was obedient to His Father's plan and did His Father's will. It is recorded that He prayed this same prayer three times. Sometimes the Father wants us to do something that is the right thing to do but may not necessarily be something we want to do. Jesus just showed us that while He knew what the right thing to do was, He still cried out from His flesh that if it was possible, could He not do it? We can ask God for guidance and strength when we are put in a position to do something that we don't necessarily want to do but know deep in our souls that it is something we have to do. He will minister to you and strengthen you. In Luke 22:42–43 Jesus prayed, "'Father, if it is Your will, take this cup away from Me; nevertheless, not My will, but Yours, be done.' Then an angel appeared to Him from heaven, strengthening Him." Jesus is our example of how to properly conduct our lives. When you are faced with something that seems so difficult yet you know you need to move forward with it, pray to the Father. He will strengthen you.

Jesus allowed the leaders to take Him into custody. They led Him away to be interrogated, beaten, and bloodied. Everyone who had declared allegiance to Him scattered. They denied knowing who He was and hid from sight so as to not be found. He was left to suffer alone, without any support from His closest friends. In a mock trial, they found Him guilty and petitioned Rome to crucify Him. The Roman prefect had Him scourged, or flogged thoroughly. Scourging was a legal preliminary to every Roman execution, and only women and Roman senators or soldiers (except in cases of desertion) were exempt. The usual instrument was a short whip with several single or braided leather thongs of variable lengths, in which small iron balls or sharp pieces of sheep bones were tied at intervals. For scourging, the man was stripped of his clothing, and his hands were tied to an upright post. The back, buttocks, and legs were flogged either by two soldiers or by one who alternated positions. The severity of the scourging depended on the disposition of the soldiers, and it was intended to weaken the victim to a state just short of collapse or death. As the Roman soldiers repeatedly struck the victim's back with full force, the iron balls would cause deep contusions, and the leather thongs and sheep bones would cut into the skin and subcutaneous tissues. Then, as the flogging continued, the lacerations would tear into the underlying skeletal muscles and produce quivering ribbons of bleeding flesh. Pain and blood loss generally set the stage for circulatory shock. The extent of blood loss may well have determined how long the victim would survive on the cross. After the scourging, the soldiers often taunted their victims. When the scourging of Jesus was completed, Pilate presented Him to the Jewish leaders and told them that he could find no fault in Him. That wasn't good enough; they wanted Him dead. The Jewish leaders incited the crowd to shout out for Him to be crucified. After a while, Pilate finally consented but not before symbolically washing his hands of this sentence. Jesus was paraded through town, beaten and naked, forced to carry His own cross up to a hill called Golgotha. He was so weak from the beatings that the soldiers compelled a man named Simon to carry His cross for Him, walking behind Jesus as He traveled through the city. This is found in Luke 23:26. Once at Golgotha (Calvary), He was nailed to the cross and lifted up into the air. He only lasted about six hours up there before He finally gave up His spirit. His blood was spent, providing the price required to redeem humankind. Even in His dying words He cried out, "Father forgive them, for they know not what they do."

Now His Spirit would go into the depths of hell to finalize the payment. The earth itself reacted to His death. The skies were darkened to hide the hideousness of His death. A great earthquake occurred at the moment His spirit left His body, and the veil that separated the Holy of Holies within the temple was torn in two from top to bottom. This signified God Himself tearing asunder the veil that separated humankind from Him. Jesus's body was taken down and placed into a tomb that didn't belong to Him. There was turmoil everywhere. This man who preached the good news was now dead. His followers were scattered, and the entire region was in chaos. The next day was the Sabbath, so no one of Jewish descent did anything that day. By their own laws, no work was to be done. Only attendance at the temple and worship to God was to be done.

While it was still dark the day following the Sabbath, there were women followers of Jesus that came to the tomb. It was a Mary who witnessed the birth of Jesus as a baby, and now another Mary was about to witness His birth again, only this one was none like one that had ever occurred before. As recorded in Matthew 28, Mary Magdalene and the other Mary came to the tomb, and there was a great earthquake, for an angel of the Lord descended from heaven and came and rolled back the stone from the door and sat on it. The angel said to the women:

> *Do not be afraid, for I know that you seek Jesus who was crucified. He is not here; for He is risen, as He said. Come, see the place where the Lord lay. And go quickly and tell His disciples that He is risen from the dead, and indeed he is going before you into Galilee; there you will see Him.*

God the Father called His Son's Spirit out of the depths of hell, and it came again into His body. He was resurrected from the dead, and His body was transformed to one that was immortal. He was now the firstborn from the dead. His Spirit went into hell, fulfilling the debt. He took the authority that Adam had surrendered to Satan, and now Jesus possessed that authority. In Matthew 28:18, Jesus declared, "All authority has been given to Me in heaven and on earth." Jesus redeemed us to the Father. Now we can go boldly before Him, just like a child can go before its earthly father, and ask for whatever we will, and because of Jesus, it will be granted to us. Our only requirement is that we recognize that Jesus is the Son of God, that He died and was resurrected from death and is now seated on the right hand of God the Father.

This is very simple and easy to do. That was Jesus's mission on earth, to restore the simplicity of God's love. Romans 10:8–11 says:

> *But what does it say? "The word is near you, in your mouth and in your heart" (that is, the word of faith which we preach): that if you confess with your mouth the Lord Jesus and believe in your heart that God has raised Him from the dead, you will be saved. For with the heart one believes unto righteousness, and with the mouth confession is made unto salvation. For the Scripture says, "Whoever believes on Him will not be put to shame."*

God the Father wants so very much to restore His relationship with you. He wants to have conversations with you anytime you want, about anything that you want. If you have never experienced this and you really want to have that personal, one-on-one relationship with Him, it is very easy to do. You can say these words and begin that journey to growing a very special closeness to Him that only a real Father can give.

Jesus is the key to having that relationship with the Father. If you don't know Him as your savior, here is how to make it happen. Just say the following out loud.

Heavenly Father, I come to You in the name of Jesus. Your Word says, "Whosoever will call on the name of the Lord will be saved" and "If I will confess with my mouth that Jesus is Lord and believe in my heart that God raised Him from the dead, I will be saved." Father, I take You at Your word. I confess that Jesus is Lord. I believe that You raised Him from the dead. I ask You to come and be Lord of my heart. I thank You for coming into my heart, and I thank You for Your Holy Spirit as You have promised.

If you have spoken these words out loud and believed them in your heart, you are now a new creation. Things are about to change in your life in a big way. Find a church, and attend and read the Bible every day. Rejoice, for your redemption is drawing near.